**New Directions for
Child and Adolescent
Development**

Reed W. Larson
Lene Arnett Jensen
EDITORS-IN-CHIEF

William Damon
FOUNDING EDITOR

Respect and Disrespect: Cultural and Developmental Origins

David W. Shwalb
Barbara J. Shwalb
EDITORS

D1521964

Number 114 • Winter 2006
Jossey-Bass
San Francisco

RESPECT AND DISRESPECT: CULTURAL AND DEVELOPMENTAL ORIGINS
David W. Shwalb, Barbara J. Shwalb (eds.)
New Directions for Child and Adolescent Development, no. 114
Reed W. Larson, Lene Arnett Jensen, Editors-in-Chief

Microfilm copies of issues and articles are available in 16mm and 35mm, as well as microfiche in 105mm, through University Microfims, Inc., 300 North Zeeb Road, Ann Arbor, Michigan 48106-1346.

ISSN 1520-3247   electronic ISSN 1534-8687

NEW DIRECTIONS FOR CHILD AND ADOLESCENT DEVELOPMENT is part of The Jossey-Bass Education Series and is published quarterly by Wiley Subscription Services, Inc., a Wiley company, at Jossey-Bass, 989 Market Street, San Francisco, California 94103-1741. Periodicals postage paid at San Francisco, California, and at additional mailing offices. Postmaster: Send address changes to New Directions for Child and Adolescent Development, Jossey-Bass, 989 Market Street, San Francisco, CA 94103-1741.

New Directions for Child and Adolescent Development is indexed in PsycInfo, Biosciences Information Service, Current Index to Journals in Education (ERIC), Psychological Abstracts, and Sociological Abstracts.

SUBSCRIPTIONS cost $90.00 for individuals and $240.00 for institutions, agencies, and libraries.

EDITORIAL CORRESPONDENCE should be e-mailed to the editors-in-chief: Reed W. Larson (larsonr@uiuc.edu) and Lene Arnett Jensen (ljensen@clarku.edu).

Jossey-Bass Web address: www.josseybass.com

CONTENTS

1

Respect and disrespect are topics that researchers and theorists have neglected, yet they are of great interest to the public and professionals in family and school settings. They are also ideal topics for both cross-cultural and mainstream developmental studies.

Research and Theory on Respect and Disrespect: Catching Up with the Public and Practitioners

David W. Shwalb, Barbara J. Shwalb

Respect has been called "the single most powerful ingredient in nourishing relationships and creating a just society" (Lawrence-Lightfoot, 2000, p. 13), and yet it has been the target of very little systematic research. Parents, educators, researchers, children, and adolescents in many societies all note with alarm a growing problem of disrespect and a decline in respect for self and others. Is this disturbing trend a universal problem? To answer this question, we must study the cultural origins of respect and disrespect. How and when do respect and disrespect develop in childhood or adolescence? The answer to this question will help scientists, practitioners, and the general public understand why disrespect becomes a problem and how we can foster respect in young people.

We believe that respectful children and adolescents tend to become respectful, civil, and tolerant adults. Conversely, we assume that the origins of incivility, disrespect, intolerance, and other problems of adults are formed in childhood and adolescence. For example, lacking respect for parents or authorities, a young child may not be receptive to what one can learn at home or at school. Brought up to disrespect other people based on social status or race, a child may become prejudiced. With a lack of respect for

---

This volume is dedicated with respect and gratitude to the memory of our mentor and friend, Irving Sigel.

NEW DIRECTIONS FOR CHILD AND ADOLESCENT DEVELOPMENT, no. 114, Winter 2006 © Wiley Periodicals, Inc.
Published online in Wiley InterScience (www.interscience.wiley.com) • DOI: 10.1002/cad.171

oneself, an adolescent may develop a negative self-concept and lack respect for others. Growing up with disrespect for older people, a young adult may be unable to keep a job in the work world that requires understanding the authority of others. Respect and disrespect indeed have relevance across the entire life span, for instance, in respect for the elderly and respect for the dignity of the dying.

Respect may indeed be the glue that binds people together and holds together one's self-concept. If respect is akin to "positive regard" (Rogers, 1961), it is the belief that enables one to value other people, institutions, and traditions. And disrespect may be the agent that dissolves relationships and fosters hostility and cynicism. All of the preceding suggests to us that respect is essential in a civil society and crucial to positive human relations. Disrespect, although we will suggest later that it is not the opposite of respect, may be one reason for incivility and polarization between individuals and between groups.

Each chapter author in this volume shares a common interest in respect and disrespect as important developmental phenomena. Each also shares the view that we cannot understand development without studying the various layers of context (of which culture is only one layer) within which development takes place. This volume presents groundbreaking research on respect and disrespect in a variety of populations (American, Puerto Rican, Turkish, German, Vietnamese, Cambodian, Laotian, Filipino, Thai, Japanese, and Chinese), on a variety of age groups (children, adolescents, adults), and in school, family, community, and societal contexts, as studied by specialists in the fields of psychology, family studies, sociology, and teacher education.

The chapter authors regard respect at times as an antecedent, correlate, and consequence of development. The research groups consider respect as, alternatively, a meaning system, an outcome of parent-child communication in the acculturation process, and a mediator of social competence in peer groups. In addition, this volume considers the development of disrespect, a phenomenon that has never been directly studied in previous psychological research. The chapters address four sets of questions to advance our understanding of respect and disrespect:

1. *Definition.* What are respect and disrespect? We know that these words are important to people everywhere. But as scientists, we want to know how are they related to or different from (as antecedents, outcomes, or correlates) other relevant psychological constructs, such as morality, prosocial behavior, altruism, obedience, and liking for others. Are respect and disrespect polar opposites of each other, or are they independent or dichotomous constructs? Is it possible to define these concepts in a way that generalizes across cultural groups or is appropriate for different research methodologies? We must clarify our terminology if we are to build a body of knowledge relevant to scholars across fields, including the social sciences, humanities, and applied disciplines such as nursing and educational studies.

NEW DIRECTIONS FOR CHILD AND ADOLESCENT DEVELOPMENT • DOI: 10.1002/cad

2. *Measurement.* How should we measure respect and disrespect? Researchers with different approaches have thus far used various measures, alternatively, to emphasize behavioral, cognitive, or attitudinal manifestations of respect and disrespect. Diversity of measurement is appropriate for studying phenomena that are important across disciplines, but at some point, we must be able to compare the findings of different research groups.

3. *Context.* Are respectful and disrespectful behavior, thinking, and traits situation specific, do they depend on the giver or recipient of the respect or disrespect, and what affective variables have an interface with person and situation variables? In the course of their development, do respect and disrespect take different form or function in family versus school contexts, depending on the recipient of one's behavior or attitude? It is important to study whether respectfulness is a general personality trait or whether training to respect at home, for example, may not generalize to children's attitudes and behavior at school. Analysis of contextual factors will help to better understand which settings are most appropriate for interventions to promote respect.

4. *Culture.* What aspects of respect and disrespect vary between or within cultures, and which have cross-cultural generality? Do they have the same or different meaning to people in various subcultures or language groups? Examination of respect and disrespect in several cultural and ethnic groups may reveal both cultural specificity and universality.

Background

The authors of three of the chapters took part in a 2005 symposium, "Respect and Valuing of Others," at the Atlanta convention of the Society for Research in Child Development (SRCD). The symposium's discussant (García Coll, 2005) referred to this set of papers as "first-generation" research and cautioned that we must distinguish between respect and disrespect and other behavior of people who also happen to be respectful or disrespectful. Another characteristic of the SRCD symposium papers was that they all were based on ongoing programmatic research. In contrast, a review of previous readings on the topic of respect (prior to the work of the chapter authors) consisted usually of one paper by each respective author (for example, Dillon, 1992; Lightfoot, 2000; and Yelsma and Yelsma, 1998).

Conducting our own research at several public schools, we realized that while respect and disrespect attract little attention from developmental scientists, practitioners and the general public value the attention of researchers. These professionals face the dilemma of how to handle a decline of respect and growth of disrespect on a daily basis. We scholars need to catch up with what parents, teachers, children, and adolescents know already: respect and disrespect are fundamentally important aspects of the experiences of children and adolescents.

The 2005 SRCD symposium discussant also remarked that respect seemed more important outside mainstream American culture, but is this

NEW DIRECTIONS FOR CHILD AND ADOLESCENT DEVELOPMENT • DOI: 10.1002/cad

true? Is respect less central to the values of middle-class American culture than elsewhere? Is it accidental that most recent research on this topic has emphasized a sociocultural viewpoint? There is no reason that first-generation research must begin in the United States. As has been pointed out by indigenous psychology (Kim, 2001), the study of non-Western cultures can reveal or redefine independent or dependent variables previously unnoticed in Western research.

An Agenda for Research on Respect and Disrespect

We propose the following thematic and methodological priorities to researchers who continue to pioneer in this new topic area.

Applied Research. We who conduct research on the sociocultural origins of respect and disrespect need to study the work of intervention specialists. We believe that developmental studies should promote human welfare (Miller, 1969), and the subject matter of this volume is well suited to such a goal. School teachers and school administrators may appreciate our attention to the issues of respect and disrespect out of their frustration in the face of everyday disrespect. But some of us researchers operate unaware of the contributions of practitioners. In the published literature, there are already several programs that foster respect and combat disrespect in school settings. These applied programs (see Aronson, 2001; Borba, 2001; Lickona, 2004; Watson, 2003) were devised by experts in the social sciences and classroom research with an awareness of developmental issues. Respect is typically one of several outcomes fostered by their interventions. For instance, Lickona (2004) refers to respect as one of the "Fourth and Fifth Rs" along with responsibility, and Borba (2001) calls respect one of seven "essential virtues" that form the basis of morality. These authors in turn would benefit from the sociocultural perspectives of this volume's chapter authors.

Self-Respect. An important construct that is not considered in this volume is self-respect, a concept that requires attention in relation to self-esteem and interpersonal respect. This volume's chapter authors instead have focused on interpersonal respect. Nevertheless, this does not negate recognition that the intrapersonal respect is an important developmental outcome, correlate, and antecedent. As Borba (2001, p. 120) wrote about American school children, "Decrease in self-respect leads them to act disrespectfully toward others as well as themselves. . ." Baumeister, Smart, and Boden (1996) indicated that individuals with inflated high self-esteem may react to threats with violence or aggression. In such a case, high self-esteem leads to disrespectful acts. Such a controversy shows the need for additional research on the connections between self-respect, self-esteem, respect for others, and esteem of others.

Disrespect. Most of this volume is concerned with respect, whereas disrespect is usually a footnote or a secondary concern, sometimes noted only because we as editors asked the writers to "say something" about disrespect. But if we look at real-world concerns, what arouses the passions of teachers, parents, school administrators, professors, and students in daily life may be more about disrespect than respect. We therefore give disrespect equal emphasis in our own research and hope that future research will accord disrespect the attention it deserves. Our data suggest that to children, disrespect may not simply be the absence of respect. We are, for example, interested in connections between the concepts of respect and prosocial behavior, and between disrespect and aggression.

Respect and Disrespect as Distinct and Multifaceted. Respect and disrespect have affective components, and one reason that we typically study these concepts separately is that people tend to think of them as opposites. Respect is usually viewed as desirable and positive, whereas disrespect often is viewed as negative and undesirable. But under some circumstances, a bully may gain respect among peers by harming others or gain self-respect because of his or her dominant status (Baumeister, Smart, and Boden, 1996). In such settings, respect is self-enhancing yet socially undesirable. In such instances respect is not an example of "positive psychology." In addition, it is possible to respect a person's public behavior and disrespect the same person's private behavior. Future research on contextual influences may help us better understand the complex interplay among the cognitive, affective, and behavioral components of respect and disrespect.

Theory Building. In addition to these concerns, researchers in this area must be concerned with theoretical issues. We need more research on the processes and origins of the development of respect and disrespect. There is no consensus on a theoretical foundation for research on respect and disrespect, although some writers cite Piaget's work (1932, 1977). The chapters in this volume all focus on cultural issues, but they have various theoretical approaches. Some (Chapter Two) begin with a clearly stated set of respectful dimensions, while others (Chapters Four and Five) conduct research with the goal of showing how definitions themselves compare among cultural groups. Each of these research teams has explored respect as an important issue in the cultures where they did their research. This volume brings their work together on paper, but another challenge ahead is to foster communication among researchers on theoretical and methodological issues.

Future Research on Respect and Disrespect. Finally, we hope to see more research on respect and disrespect across a wider range of subcultures. Psychological behavior, thought, and emotion in every society and subculture are affected by cultural influences, whether one is in the minority or majority. It is most important that the future study of respect and disrespect should not be a topic reserved for researchers interested in cultural influences.

Introduction to the Chapters

Chapter Two, by Robin Harwood, Alev Yalcinkaya, Banu Citlak, and Birgit Leyendecker, extends Harwood's pioneering work on "proper demeanor" (Harwood, Miller, and Lucca Irizarry, 1995) to two immigrant populations.

NEW DIRECTIONS FOR CHILD AND ADOLESCENT DEVELOPMENT • DOI: 10.1002/cad

They show that dimensions of respect first observed in Latino American culture ("proper interpersonal behavior," respect that is "lived publicly in relation to a larger community," and respect in family relations) are relevant to other populations and are also a useful mirror on respect across generations and between immigrant and host culture values. It is impressive that these researchers make compelling interpretations about development across generations, societies, and minority and majority cultures, all in one study.

Chapter Three, by Carl Bankston and Danielle Hidalgo, is a cultural, historical, and sociological analysis of American immigrant and refugee populations from five Southeast Asian cultures. They reveal both similarities and differences in the impact of culture-of-origin concepts of respect on cross-generational acculturation processes in school and family settings. Bankston and Hidalgo show that immigrant versus refugee status and the socioeconomic strata in which acculturation takes place are critical variables that mediate between respect and the adaptation and school achievement of children and adolescents. They report on several additional manifestations of respect (hierarchy-related status, filial piety, and physical expressions) not emphasized in Chapter Two.

In Chapter Four, Shuji Sugie and we show that the meaning and function of respect in a culture can change historically. The Japanese data are concerned chiefly with respect for teachers, parents, and the emperor of Japan. As in the previous two chapters, language in Japan is both a reflection of respect and a means of socialization of respect for others. Although Japanese culture shares its historical, religious, and ethical heritage with Chinese, Korean, and other Asian cultures, this chapter demonstrates how far Japan has diverged from its traditions in recent years. This dramatic social change is already changing the development of Japanese children and adolescents in this century with regard to respect and disrespect.

Chapter Five by Robert Cohen and his collaborators relates the development of respect to important phenomena studied in mainstream developmental psychology: peer relations and social competence. Their programmatic research shows that peer respect predicts peer relations in both the United States and China and that it appears to mediate the effects of peer liking. They also show that respect may be more of a core consideration for Chinese than American children. These authors emphasize the importance of culture for the definition, organization, and expression of respect for children's peer relations.

Our own Chapter Six is an exploration of what respect and disrespect mean in the context of changing American society. Like Sugie, we assert that respect and disrespect mean something different now than they did in past generations. More specifically, observations of children illustrate that even American data are cultural data. We propose that the trajectory of the development of respect may differ in timing from the developmental path of disrespect. This chapter suggests that we look at the two concepts separately and also look for their developmental roots in early childhood.

NEW DIRECTIONS FOR CHILD AND ADOLESCENT DEVELOPMENT • DOI: 10.1002/cad

Finally, Chapter Seven by Jin Li provides a summary and commentary about how the other chapters described what respect may entail, how it may function, and how it may emerge in children. She suggests that the diverse populations and methods represented in this volume are a strong point. Li relates the findings of several chapters to her own research on "ought-respect" (universal) and "affect-respect" (context-specific) and concludes that there is a need for further conceptualization and cross-cultural research on this new research topic.

This volume is relevant to the interests and research of scholars in family studies, education, nursing, and cultural area studies and developmental scientists interested in moral development, conceptual development, social and personality development, cross-cultural and intracultural comparisons, educational issues, and parent-child relationships in childhood and adolescence. We most definitely believe that this volume is a foretelling of good things to come.

Acknowledgments

We are deeply appreciative for the encouragement from *New Directions for Child and Adolescent Development* editors-in-chief Reed Larson and Lene Jensen, who granted us an extension to complete this volume following the disruptions in Louisiana in fall 2005 from Hurricanes Katrina and Rita. We extend our warm thanks to the chapter authors for always responding thoughtfully to our suggestions and questions, and mostly for their patience. We gained in respect and liking for each of these professionals during the editorial process. We thank Ruth Chao for kindly introducing us to the editors of *New Directions*. Finally, we acknowledge our faculty colleagues and students in the Psychology Department at Southeastern Louisiana University for their support.

References

Aronson, E. *Nobody Left to Hate: Teaching Compassion After Columbine.* New York: Owl Books, 2001.

Baumeister, R., Smart, L., and Boden, J. "Relation of Threatened Egotism to Violence and Aggression: The Dark Side of High Self-Esteem." *Psychological Review*, 1996, *103*, 5–33.

Borba, M. *Building Moral Intelligence: The Seven Essential Virtues That Teach Kids to Do the Right Thing.* San Francisco: Jossey-Bass, 2001.

Dillon, R. S. "Respect and Care: Toward Moral Integration." *Canadian Journal of Philosophy*, 1992, *22*, 105–132.

García Coll, C. Discussant's comments at the Respect and Valuing of Others symposium, biennial meetings of the Society for Research in Child Development, Atlanta, Apr. 2005.

Harwood, R. L., Miller, J. G., and Lucca Irizarry, N. *Culture and Attachment: Perceptions of the Child in Context.* New York: Guilford Press, 1995.

Kim, U. "Culture, Science, and Indigenous Psychologies: An Integrated Analysis." In D. Matsumoto (ed.), *The Handbook of Culture and Psychology.* New York: Oxford University Press, 2001.

Lawrence-Lightfoot, S. *Respect: An Exploration.* Cambridge, Mass.: Perseus, 2000.
Lickona, T. *Character Matters.* New York: Touchstone, 2004.
Lightfoot, C. "On Respect." *New Ideas in Psychology,* 2000, *18,* 177–185.
Miller, G. S. "Psychology as a Means of Promoting Human Welfare." *American Psychologist,* 1969, *24,* 1063–1075.
Piaget, J. *The Moral Judgment of the Child.* Orlando, Fla.: Harcourt, 1932.
Piaget, J. *Sociological Studies.* New York: Routledge, 1995. (Originally published 1977.)
Rogers, C. *On Becoming a Person.* Boston: Houghton Mifflin, 1961.
Watson, M. *Learning to Trust: Transforming Difficult Elementary Classrooms Through Developmental Discipline.* San Francisco: Jossey-Bass, 2003.
Yelsma, P., and Yelsma, J. "Self-Esteem and Social Respect Within the High School." *Journal of Social Psychology,* 1998, *138,* 431–441.

DAVID W. SHWALB is on the faculty of the Psychology Department at Southeastern Louisiana University.

BARBARA J. SHWALB is on the faculty of the Psychology Department at Southeastern Louisiana University. The Shwalbs received their Ph.D.s from the University of Michigan (Developmental Psychology; Combined Program in Education and Psychology) and have co-edited two books (Japanese Childrearing, 1996; Applied Developmental Psychology, 2005), two books published in Japanese, and special journal issues of Evaluation in Education (1985), International Journal of Educational Research (1996), and Journal of Applied Developmental Psychology (1998).

NEW DIRECTIONS FOR CHILD AND ADOLESCENT DEVELOPMENT • DOI: 10.1002/cad

The cultural patterning of respect is examined in two first- and second-generation migrant groups: Puerto Rican mothers in Connecticut and Turkish mothers in Bochum, Germany. Cultural and generational influences were found for three aspects of respect: proper interpersonal behavior, relations within the family, and esteem within the community.

Exploring the Concept of Respect Among Turkish and Puerto Rican Migrant Mothers

Robin L. Harwood, Alev Yalçinkaya, Banu Citlak, Birgit Leyendecker

Individualism and autonomy have been treated in numerous works over the past two decades as primary analytical dimensions of culture that influence parents' child-rearing beliefs and values (Harkness, Raeff, and Super, 2000). However, cultural analyses of the concept of respect have remained underspecified in the literature. Often subsumed under the larger rubric of interdependence (see Harwood, Miller, Carlson, and Leyendecker, 2002), respect is itself a complex concept that needs unpacking by researchers (Harwood, 2006). A closer analysis of the concept of respect and how it may be patterned across different cultural groups is a timely undertaking.

Respect is a multidimensional construct. Harwood, Miller, and Lucca Irizarry (1995) described three dimensions of respectfulness that emerged in their work with Puerto Rican mothers in both Puerto Rico and Connecticut: (1) proper interpersonal behavior that is important to harmonious relationships, such as being polite, well behaved, and well mannered; (2) a dimension that implicitly acknowledges the extent to which one's life is lived publicly in relation to a larger community, that is, "one's life is lived under the watchful eyes of an observing community that has the power to

This research was made possible through a grant to Robin L. Harwood from the National Institute of Child Health and Human Development.

offer either love and acceptance or rejection and pain. The esteem of the community is paramount, and such esteem is granted only when one comports oneself with *respeto*" (Harwood, Miller, and Lucca Irizarry, 1995, p. 99); and (3) a third dimension that focuses on relations within the family and is concerned primarily with respect toward parents and other older relatives, as well as fulfillment of family role obligations (Citlak and others, 2006). In this chapter, we examine these three dimensions of respect as expressed in the child-rearing beliefs and values of migrant Puerto Rican and Turkish mothers.

Child-Rearing Beliefs and Values: Two Populations

Mothers' child-rearing beliefs and values have been found to reflect broad cultural scripts regarding definitions of desirable child-rearing outcomes and adult social competence (Harwood, Miller, and Lucca Irizarry, 1995). These broad cultural scripts influence child-rearing practices and have shown considerable variation across different groups (Harkness and Super, 1996). In the case of migrant populations, child-rearing beliefs serve as an index regarding the extent to which parents' culture-of-origin values may persist across generations in their host culture, versus the extent to which they may change in response to new cultural influences.

Puerto Ricans in the United States. Puerto Ricans are the second largest Latino group in the United States (In 2000, Mexican Americans were 58 percent and Puerto Ricans 10 percent of all Latinos). In the Northeast U.S., Puerto Ricans are the largest group, accounting for nearly 40 percent of the total regional Latino population in 2000. Migration to and from the mainland constitutes a critical element of Puerto Rican life today. As Alarcón, Erkut, García Coll, and Vázquez García (1994) observe, Puerto Ricans "have the unique status of being native born Americans who are immigrants because of culture and geography, not legal status. Having no restrictions, they travel back and forth from the island to the mainland" (p. 2). The 2000 Census reported over 7 million Puerto Ricans, half (48 percent) of whom lived on the U.S. mainland (U.S. Census Bureau, 2000). On the island itself, located about a thousand miles southeast of Florida, one of every four Puerto Ricans is estimated to have undergone some sort of migratory experience (Lucca Irizarry and Pacheco, 1992), making Puerto Rican migration to and from the United States "one of the world's most sustained population displacements" (Lucca Irizarry and Pacheco, 1992, p. 226). This circular migration is likely to affect patterns of acculturation by increasing the degree of exposure to both cultures that Puerto Rican children are likely to experience (Alarcón, Erkut, García Coll, and Vázquez García, 1994).

Harwood, Miller, and Lucca Irizarry (1995) identified "Proper Demeanor" as a primary child-rearing value among working-class Puerto Rican mothers, on both the island and mainland. *Proper demeanor* is defined as "knowing the level of courtesy and decorum required in a given situation in relation to other people of a particular age, sex, and social status. The cardinal rule governing Proper demeanor in Puerto Rico is *respeto,* or respect, which will manifest itself differently in different contexts" (p. 98). Specific dimensions of interpersonal behavior related to *respeto* for children include being *obediente* (obedient), *tranquilo* (calm), *amable* (polite, gentle, kind), and *carinoso* (sweet, affectionate).

In addition to the interpersonal aspects of *respeto,* proper demeanor has a strong public dimension. Children who breach parental or community expectations regarding appropriate behavior face the potential for *vergüenza* (shame) through loss of face. Moreover, children who behave poorly shame not only themselves but also the parents, who may be seen by the community as having failed to rear their children properly (Harwood, Miller, and Lucca Irizarry, 1995). In contrast, a person who fulfills the requirements of *respeto* is *una persona de provecho* who comports him or herself with *dignidad,* a person of worth who can be trusted to fulfill obligations to others, behaves with dignity, and so gains the esteem of others in the community (Harwood, Miller, and Lucca Irizarry, 1995). Finally, proper demeanor has implications for ordering relations within the family. Respect and obedience toward parents and other elders is expected, within a context of *confianza* (trust). *Confianza* within the mother-child relationship in particular makes the child open to the parent's wisdom and guidance.

Turks in Germany. To examine whether the three dimensions of respect that we identified among Puerto Ricans would emerge as important in another migrating group, we looked at a second rapidly growing minority population: Turks in Germany. Currently Turks are the largest minority group in Germany, with almost 2 million Turkish citizens living in Germany, in addition to an unknown number of people who are German citizens with Turkish ancestry (Bundesamt für Statistik, 2006). Originally Turks were recruited in the early 1960s by the German government as guest workers, whereas today the majority of Turks migrate to Germany for purposes of family reunification.

With regard to the three dimensions of respect identified by Harwood, Miller, and Lucca Irizarry (1995), traditional Turkish culture has been characterized as endorsing respect in interpersonal relationships, particularly toward authority and for older people (Kagitcibasi and Sunar, 1992). The continuing relevance of the traditional proverb, "Respect the elders and love the younger ones," is seen in the fact that as Turkish children grow older, they are expected to be respectful, obedient, and receptive to the authority of their elders (Imamoglu, 1987). Young children, however, are typically treated with indulgence, in that they are not expected to follow rules, and even misbehavior is often tolerated (Pfluger-Schindlbeck, 1989). Indulgence is generally limited to the first five to seven years of life and is likely to be gradually replaced by a parenting style that is demanding and strict. For example, Kagitcibasi (1996) reported that most Turkish mothers perceive the interruption of an adult conversation by a child as "not tolerable."

Traditional Turkish culture places high value on close, lasting family relationships (Kagitcibasi and Sunar, 1992). As children grow older, they spend more time helping their younger siblings, parents, and extended family as needed. The traditional patterns of indulgence toward the young and respect toward elders are viewed as important in establishing strong emotional ties between the generations. These intergenerational emotional ties are in turn frequently associated with attention to familial duties and obligations (Kagitcibasi, 1996; Leyendecker, Harwood, Comparini, and Yalcinkaya, 2005). For example, Sunar and Fişek (2005) presented findings comparing Western and Turkish family patterns of the personal boundaries of each individual family member. They suggested that the strong hierarchy within the Turkish family offsets the high levels of intimacy, interdependence, and proximity, providing differentiation between family members while still allowing for interconnectedness.

In addition, previous research highlights the relevance of a clear demarcation of gender roles and hierarchy in Turkish families (Kagitcibasi and Sunar, 1992). There is strong evidence of a preference for male children among Turkish parents, especially fathers; this finding appears to account for the lower educational attainment among girls (Kagitcibasi and Sunar, 1992). This specific gender preference is related to distinct expectations parents have for their children. Specifically, sons are expected to carry on the family name and contribute to the family honor. They must also support the financial and practical needs of the family and ensure the care and security of their parents in their old age. In contrast, daughters are perceived as "the property of strangers, since once they marry, they will contribute to the welfare of their husband's family, not to their own" (Kagitcibasi and Sunar, 1992, p. 77). Research on Turkish migrants, however, suggests that these gender role differences are sensitive to opportunities in the host culture. In this respect, Turkish families in Germany may show a cross-generational trend away from gender-based constraints that result in differential academic achievement of girls and boys (Phalet and Schönpflug, 2001).

Finally, traditional Turkish culture strongly emphasizes the dimension of respect, honor, and shame within the community at large (Kongar, 2001; Pfluger-Schindlbeck, 1989; Schiffauer, 1991). Sunar and Fişek (2005) referred to *namus*, or honor, as a dominant concept valued within traditional Turkish society, a value that is maintained largely through vigilance on the part of men toward the chastity of women in the family. They also suggested that there are major differences between rural and urban groups in how people approach the concept of honor, not so much in terms of personal sin or virtue but rather as embedded in social relations.

The importance of maintaining the esteem, respect, and honor of others is also an important part of ethnic identity of Turkish migrants in diaspora, both within Germany and beyond. In particular, adherence to cultural norms regarding respect and honor creates a symbolic tie that allows access to the social network of Turkish migrants (Faist, 1999). At the same time, a shared sense of respect and honor also serves to distinguish between in-group and out-group members. For example, research on self-esteem of Turkish migrant youth (Atabay, 1994) and Turkish migrant women in Germany (Schmidt-Koddenberg, 1989) has shown that members of both groups perceive themselves as more respectful and as having a greater sense of honor than the German majority. Thus, respect appears to be an important marker of ethnic group membership for Turkish migrants living in Germany.

Contributions of This Study

Our research has explored respect as a cultural construct by examining its use in Puerto Rican and Turkish mothers' child-rearing beliefs and values. In particular, we examine three issues:

1. Are the three dimensions of respect that Harwood, Miller, and Lucca Irizarry (1995) identified useful in understanding the concept of respect across both Turkish and Puerto Rican migrant mothers?
2. What group differences exist in the patterning of respect as a construct? Are these three dimensions of respect present, absent, or emphasized differently?
3. Has the concept of respect changed or held steady among migrant mothers living in two highly industrialized, Western societies (the United States and Germany), both across the two generations and cross-nationally?

In examining these questions, we hope to begin to unpack some of the cultural, developmental, and psychological complexity of this understudied but important construct.

Method

In this section we present background on the participants and validity and reliability procedures used in this study.

Participants. Sixty-four Puerto Rican (twenty-six first-generation, thirty-eight second-generation) and fifty Turkish (twenty-five first- and twenty-five second-generation) mothers participated in the study. The Puerto Rican mothers were living in the greater Hartford area in Connecticut in the United States, and the Turkish mothers lived in Bochum, in the Ruhr industrial valley in Germany. First-generation mothers were reared and educated primarily in Puerto Rico or Turkey, and spoke Spanish or Turkish as their first language. Because schooling plays an important role in the socialization process, the first generation was defined as mothers who had spent their elementary school years in Turkey or Puerto Rico, with migration to Germany or the United States after the age of twelve. The second generation was defined as women who were reared and educated primarily in the United States or Germany, with no more than six years spent living in the country of origin.

NEW DIRECTIONS FOR CHILD AND ADOLESCENT DEVELOPMENT • DOI: 10.1002/cad

Each mother had at least one child between the ages of eighteen and thirty-six months, enabling us to examine child-rearing beliefs and values using target children who were mobile and verbal enough to elicit parental concerns regarding appropriate socialization, but too young to have encountered the significant external socializing influences that exist in school, day care, or preschool settings (Tobin, Wu, and Davidson, 1989).

Similar subject recruitment procedures were employed for all groups. In Connecticut, mothers were obtained through WIC (Women Infant Child) nutrition offices, family resource centers, and other agencies serving Puerto Rican families in the greater Hartford area. In Germany, mothers were recruited through the local registration office for foreigners, as well as through agencies serving Turkish migrant populations.

As can be seen in Table 2.1, in Connecticut mothers had at least a tenth-grade education, with an average of about twelve years of schooling, the minimum required in the United States for a high school diploma. In Germany, ten years of education is the minimum requirement for high school graduation, with some additional schooling necessary for work apprenticeships. The educational levels of second-generation Turkish mothers reflected this standard, with mothers averaging around eleven years of schooling. Until recently, only five years of schooling was mandatory in Turkey, making the first-generation Turkish mothers and their partners significantly lower ($p < .01$) in their educational achievement than the other three groups.

Table 2.1 also reveals significant group differences contrasting mothers across the two countries. Specifically, compared to Puerto Rican mothers, Turkish mothers were more likely ($p < .01$) to be married and living in nuclear families but less likely to work outside the home. In addition, the religious backgrounds of the mothers differed ($p < .01$), with the majority of Puerto Rican mothers identifying themselves as Christian (primarily Protestant or Catholic), and nearly all Turkish mothers identified as Muslim (primarily Sunni, the majority Muslim group in Turkey, or Alevite, the largest minority group).

Group demographic similarities were also evident. In particular, as seen in Table 2.1, mothers did not differ across the four groups in terms of age; gender distribution, age, or birth order of target child; total number of children; total household size; or age of partner. In all groups, unemployment rates among the mothers' partners were similarly high.

Procedures to Promote Cross-Cultural Validity. All interviews took place in the mothers' preferred language (Spanish, English, Turkish, or German). Several steps were taken to promote the cultural appropriateness of the research materials in the Puerto Rican and Turkish contexts. First, all research protocols were examined for cultural suitability by the first and fourth authors in consultation with Puerto Rican and Turkish cultural consultants; the protocols were revised on the basis of their comments. Complete translations were then undertaken by bilingual, bicultural graduate assistants at the University of Connecticut (Spanish and English) and Ruhr

University, Bochum (Turkish and German), then checked for preservation of meaning and cultural appropriateness by the cultural consultants.

Testing, Control, and Reliability Procedures. Interviews were conducted in mothers' homes by trained interviewers who were fluent in the mother's preferred language and blind to the study hypotheses. To ensure comprehension of the protocol, all interview items were read to mothers by the interviewers. Mothers' oral responses were written down verbatim for the majority of interview items; however, in order to facilitate mothers' open-ended responses to the questions regarding their socialization goals and migratory experiences, these portions of the interviews were audiotaped for later transcription. Coding of data from the oral interviews was performed by trained research assistants who were blind to the study hypotheses. Fifty percent of all open-ended interviews were coded independently by at least two different people to ensure reliability; an agreement level of at least .70 (Cohen's kappa) was obtained across all categories.

Procedures. Procedures were administered in mothers' homes in three sessions, each lasting two hours or less, scheduled within a four-week period. The interviews in the first session focused on mothers' parenting beliefs, practices, and social networks. In the second session, the interviewers observed the target child's activities. The final session investigated mothers' socialization goals, socioeconomic circumstances, and perceptions of the migratory experience.

In this chapter, we focus our analyses on data drawn from the Migratory Experiences Interview (MIE), a semistructured interview in which mothers answered a variety of questions regarding their migration histories and their perceptions of both the host culture and culture of origin. In addition, mothers described characteristics that they thought were particularly important in their Puerto Rican or Turkish culture and whether they considered these characteristics to be important child-rearing goals for their own children.

Content analysis was performed on mothers' open-ended responses to two questions: (1) "What kinds of things do you think Puerto Rican/Turkish parents consider very important when it comes to raising their children?" and (2) "Do you feel it is important for your own child to be [characteristic mentioned in question 1]? If so, why do you think this is a good quality for your child to have?" Although mothers generated a range of responses to these questions, in this chapter we focus only on their responses relevant to the concept of respect.

Turkish and Puerto Rican mothers' responses were coded into three areas:

• Eight categories representing respectful interpersonal behaviors, which included all responses mentioning (1) the importance of respect for elders and (2) for one another, including (3) self-respect as an important example for children, (4) respectful behaviors such as giving up one's seat

Table 2.1. Demographic Characteristics of Surveyed Families

	Puerto Rican Generation 1 (n = 26)	Puerto Rican Generation 2 (n = 38)	Turkish Generation 1 (n = 25)	Turkish Generation 2 (n = 25)	p
Mother's age (years)	26.4	25.3	27.7	28.2	
Mother's education (years)	11.7	12.1	7.6	11.0	**
Religious background (percentage)					**
None	7.7	10.5	4.0	4.0	
Protestant	46.2	15.8	0	0	
Catholic	30.8	55.3	0	0	
Sunni	0	0	62.5	76.0	
Alevite	0	0	25.0	16.0	
Shiite	0	0	4.2	0	
Other	15.4	18.4	4.2	4.2	
Age of target child (months)	24.6	23.9	26.2	24.1	
Percentage firstborn	34.6	44.7	60.0	52.0	
Percentage female	46.2	42.1	52.0	52.0	

Total number of children	2.1	2.0	1.6
Total household size	3.9	4.0	3.6
Percentage of mothers employed	50.0	55.3	24.0 **
Number of hours worked per week	33.9	31.2	20.6 **
Percentage of mothers living with partner	65.4	63.2	96.0 **
Percentage married	38.5	23.7	96.0 **
Partner's education	11.8	12.0	10.5 **
Partner's age (years)	29.4	29.0	31.7
Percentage of partners unemployed	17.6	20.8	20.0
Number of hours worked per week	43.1	40.5	45.0
Family composition			**
Percentage nuclear family	65.4	47.4	96.0
Percentage single parent	23.1	18.4	4.0
Percentage extended family	11.5	18.4	0.0
Percentage living with other adults 0.0	15.8	4.0	0.0

$* = p < .05.$ $** = p < .01.$

to an older person or not interrupting an adult conversation, (5) being obedient and calm, (6) being well mannered and polite, (7) not talking back, and (8) respect as an important quality without further elaboration.

• Three categories representing relations within the family: (1) respect for parents, (2) the importance of family ties and obligations, and (3) the importance (or not) of maintaining traditional gender roles within the family.

• Five categories representing participation in and esteem within the larger community: (1) respect as necessary for one's future success and well-being, (2) respect as defining a good person, (3) the importance (or not) of maintaining family honor and virginity, (4) the importance of religious beliefs and observance, and (5) the importance of maintaining one's cultural heritage and traditions.

Results

Chi-square analyses were performed on the percentages of mothers indicating that they planned to encourage their own child to develop qualities relevant to each of the coding categories. As can be seen in Table 2.2, the overwhelming majority of mothers in all four groups mentioned at least one of the three dimensions of respect in response to the question regarding culturally desirable characteristics and whether they were also encouraging these characteristics in their own children. In addition, all three dimensions of respect identified by Harwood, Miller, and Lucca Irizarry (1995) were present across all four groups and accounted for the range of mothers' responses on this topic.

The dimension of respect that was identified as important to mothers in all four groups was participation in and esteem within the larger community. In particular, participation in the migrant community through the maintenance of cultural heritage was viewed as similarly important by all four groups. This was true of both the maintenance of cultural identity and the maintenance of specific customs and traditions:

> Because we are Puerto Rican, we don't want our culture to disappear. Although we are in another country, [we want] for our culture to be maintained forever. This is like a chain. [Puerto Rican first generation]

> I never forget religious holidays. They are special days for me—religious holidays, circumcision ceremonies, weddings, are special days for me. I definitely visit elders during those days. I buy my children new clothing and I try to make them feel it is a special holiday. [Turkish first generation]

However, there were differences among the four groups in the patterning of these dimensions. For example, although the majority of mothers in each group mentioned the importance of participation in and esteem within

Table 2.2. Percentage of Mothers Discussing Desirability of Characteristics in Relation to Their Own Child

Characteristics Mentioned by Mothers as Desirable	Puerto Rican Generation 1 (n = 26)	Puerto Rican Generation 2 (n = 38)	Turkish Generation 1 (n = 25)	Turkish Generation 2 (n = 25)	p
Three dimensions overall	84.6	86.8	92.0	96.0	
Proper interpersonal behavior	42.3	39.5	80.0	60.0	**
Respect for elders	26.9	7.9	32.0	44.0	**
Respect for one another	19.2	10.5	4.0	0	
Respectful behaviors	7.7	2.6	12.0	20.0	
Self-respect	11.5	0	4.0	0	
Obedient/calm	3.8	10.5	36.0	12.0	**
Well mannered/polite	7.7	15.8	12.0	4.0	
Avoid talking back	0	7.9	4.0	0	
Respect (not elaborated)	0	5.3	12.0	0	
Relations within the family	38.5	34.2	56.0	64.0	
Respect for parents	23.1	13.2	12.0	24.0	
Importance of family ties	26.9	21.1	36.0	28.0	
Gender roles	3.8	5.3	20.0	40.0	**
Participation in and esteem within the community	73.1	55.3	60.0	72.0	
Respect necessary for future success and well being	26.9	13.2	20.0	8.0	
Respect defines a good person	11.5	10.5	8.0	8.0	
Maintain honor/virginity	3.8	2.6	12.0	24.0	*
Maintain religion	42.3	26.3	16.0	44.0	
Maintain cultural heritage and traditions	38.5	28.9	28.0	32.0	

* = p < .05. ** = p < .01.

the community, second-generation Turkish mothers in particular were more likely than Puerto Rican mothers to discuss family honor and the importance of a girl's virginity in this context:

> For women or for girls, honor [is important]. . . . That they should get married as a virgin—actually to not [even] have been seen openly with a guy. . . . . . For me [it is] is not important that she gets married as a virgin, but I would not want that she keeps changing relationships either. She needs to be careful with that. [Turkish second generation]

Among first-generation mothers, respect was considered essential to their child's future success:

> Respect is very important. Then they can succeed, wherever they go. They have a larger network. They can get into dialogue with more people. . . . If she is respectful, everyone will like her. [Turkish first generation]

> If she learns *respeto,* if we instill *respeto* since she's little, then when she is older, she will have it. She will be used to respecting people, and will succeed in life. [Puerto Rican, first generation]

Intriguing group differences were also observed with regard to religion. For example, religion seemed most closely related to participation in and esteem within the community for first-generation Puerto Rican and second-generation Turkish mothers:

> So I want him to show respect, to have certain goals clearly even though we are in Germany, and about Islam, to be confronted with our religion, to have our own holidays, for him to read the Koran occasionally, for him to pray possibly, so he simply learns all of this. . . . One has to lead children. [Turkish second generation]

> A child that you teach respect, he is learning it before you, in other words you are respecting yourself and so is he, because you are giving them an example. . . . And in giving them a good religious base it is like a compliment so that your child learns to respect their neighbor, other people, and his parents, who are the ones he is more in contact with. [Puerto Rican first generation]

There were also group differences in cultural patterning with regard to the two other dimensions of respect, with Turkish mothers more likely than Puerto Rican mothers to spontaneously mention that proper interpersonal behaviors were important cultural qualities that they were encouraging in their own children:

> When we are among people and my daughter, she is five, is sitting on a couch, and an elderly woman comes in and she keeps sitting and does not get up. I cannot tolerate this. Then she can say, "Lady come, I can stand up, you

sit down"—or in the train, or so—to show respect towards adults. [Turkish second generation]

Interestingly, whereas second-generation Turkish mothers placed strong emphasis on respect for elders within this dimension, first-generation Puerto Rican mothers, compared to Turkish mothers, placed relatively greater emphasis on respect for one another:

> To teach him that in my house he needs to remember that here there has to be mutual respect. I respect him and he has to respect me, in all—in what he asks for, in his behavior, and everything. . . . . When one gives him mutual respect, he learns to respect others, and lets others make their own decisions, and that he knows he can't make decisions for the whole world. [Puerto Rican first generation]

With regard to the dimension of relations within the family, mothers across all four groups mentioned the importance of family ties:

> Respect is important for me, but as a harmonious togetherness. Family ties. She should—I mean I find [it] important for my child—that she knows, that she feels comfortable in her family. She can take energy from the family. [Turkish second generation]

> Well, one of the things that in my family is very important is to grow up near the family. For there to be a lot of family near the children, [who] are not to be placed in day care, because grandmothers are the ones who [will] take care of them. [Puerto Rican first generation]

However, cultural patterning also arose with regard to the dimension of relations within the family, with Turkish mothers more likely to mention traditional gender roles:

> Turks segregate between girls and boys.. . . . Let's say they'll have a meal, "you are girls, you eat later, let the guys eat first." There is gender role segregation among Turks. [Turkish first generation]

Second-generation mothers often expressed ambivalence toward or even rejected such gender constraints:

> There are always differences between girls' and boys' upbringing—that girls are always socialized in such a way that they find a good husband. . . . For boys, that they have more freedom—although this [gender roles] is partially changed, it still exists. . . . . There is a difference between how girls and boys are brought up. A girl should be so and so and a boy should be so and so. . . . And I find this negative. . . . [For me, it is important] to not raise girls and boys differently. . . . [There should be the] same education, same opportunities for all children. [Turkish second generation]

NEW DIRECTIONS FOR CHILD AND ADOLESCENT DEVELOPMENT • DOI: 10.1002/cad

Discussion

Our study confirmed the view that respect is a multidimensional construct. The term *proper demeanor,* introduced by Harwood (1992), captured the multidimensionality of this construct, in that it comprises dimensions related to proper interpersonal behavior, the ordering of family relations and obligations, and participation in and esteem within the larger community. Each of these three dimensions was present in the responses of first- and second-generation mothers from the two cultural groups.

It is important to note that group differences were found in the patterning—not only of the dimensions themselves but also with regard to the specific types of responses emphasized within each dimension. For example, family honor and virginity was a stronger component of the community esteem dimension among the Turkish (particularly the second generation) than Puerto Rican mothers. Similarly, with regard to proper interpersonal relations, respect for elders was mentioned more by second-generation Turkish mothers, whereas respect for one another was emphasized more by first-generation Puerto Rican mothers.

Generational differences were noteworthy in that they did not follow a simple pattern of assimilation toward the host culture. That is, traditional values related to respect or proper demeanor did not necessarily weaken in the second compared to the first generations. Turkish mothers were particularly likely to belie the expectation that over time, mothers would move away from the pattern of their cultures of origin. For example, although emphasis on respect for elders decreased among second-generation Puerto Ricans, it increased among second-generation Turkish mothers. Emphases on respect for parents, gender roles, family honor and virginity, and maintenance of religion showed similar increases among Turkish second-generation mothers.

Therefore, although dimensions of respect remained generally important for second-generation Puerto Rican mothers, it was noteworthy that for many second-generation Turkish mothers, these dimensions increased dramatically in importance. It is possible that although both Turks and Puerto Ricans begin their sojourns in the United States and Germany as visible members of a minority culture, second-generation Turks may experience more alienation from the surrounding German culture than second-generation Puerto Ricans experience in relation to the mainstream U.S. culture. Such alienation may lead to the deliberate cultivation of an in-group identity, marked by an emphasis on Islamic religious identity and of respect for parents and other elders. In other cases, second-generation Turks seem preoccupied with separating themselves from specific cultural traditions that they grew up with, especially the restrictive gender roles and importance of maintaining female chastity before marriage. Perhaps the social conservatism of many first-generation Turkish immigrants creates a stark contrast for the second generation between the strict separation of

NEW DIRECTIONS FOR CHILD AND ADOLESCENT DEVELOPMENT • DOI: 10.1002/cad

gender roles in the migrant community versus the relative flexibility of gender roles observable in mainstream German society.

We need to further explore respect as a multidimensional construct that shows differential patterning across a variety of groups. For example, group differences in the use of the concept of respect among middle-class European Americans as compared to Puerto Rican and other minority groups deserve special consideration in order to determine whether these dimensions are present across diverse groups. In addition, comparisons between the host culture and the culture of origin in future postmigration generations will provide greater insight into the dynamnic, changing quality of the consruct of respect, enabling us to answer a variety of questions. Will change in future generations increase the similarities between migrant and host culture mothers' conceptions of respect? Is change toward the host culture associated with less participation in the cultural heritage, traditions, and religion of the migrant community? To what extent and under what circumstances do a bicultural identity and child-rearing values from the culture of origin endure, perhaps alongside or in transformative combination with child-rearing values from the host culture? Finally, how are the three dimensions of respect, although analytically separate, interconnected in mothers' beliefs and practices? Future research examining the cultural patterning of the construct of respect is warranted in societies throughout the world.

References

Alarcón, O., Erkut, S., García Coll, C., and Vázquez García, H. *An Approach to Engaging in Culturally Sensitive Research on Puerto Rican Youth.* Wellesley, Mass.: Center for Research on Women, 1994.

Atabay, I. *Ist Dies Mein Land? Identitätsentwicklung Türkischer Migrantenkinder und Jugendlicher in der Bundesrepublik.* Pfaffenweiler: Centaurus-Verl.-Ges., 1994.

Bundesamt für Statistik (Federal Statistical Office and the Statistical Offices of the Länder). "Ausländische Bevölkerung nach Staatsangehörigkeit (Foreign Population by Country of Origin)." *Ausländerzentralregister* (Central Register on Foreigners). Retrieved Sept. 27, 2006, from http://www.destatis.de/Stuttgart.

Citlak, B., and others. "Long-Term Socialization Goals Among First and Second Generation Migrant Turkish and German Mothers." Unpublished manuscript, 2006.

Faist, T. "Developing Transnational Social Spaces: The Turkish German Example." In L. Pries (ed.), *Migration and Transnational Spaces.* Aldershot, U.K.: Ashgate, 1999.

Harkness, S., Raeff, C., and Super, C. M. (eds.). *Variability in the Social Construction of the Child.* New Directions for Child Development, no. 87. San Francisco: Jossey-Bass, 2000.

Harkness, S., and Super, C. M. (eds.). *Parents' Cultural Belief Systems.* New York: Guilford Press, 1996.

Harwood, R. L. "The Influence of Culturally Derived Values on Anglo and Puerto Rican Mothers' Perceptions of Attachment Behavior." *Child Development,* 1992, *63,* 822–839.

Harwood, R. L. "Multidimensional Culture and the Search for Universals." *Human Development,* 2006, *49,* 122-128.

Harwood, R. L., Miller, A. M., Carlson, V. J., and Leyendecker, B. "Child-Rearing Beliefs and Practices During Feeding Among Middle-Class Puerto Rican and Anglo Mother-Infant Pairs." In J. M. Contreras, K. A. Kerns, and A. M. Neal-Barnett (eds.), *Latino Children and Families in the United States.* Westport, Conn.: Praeger, 2002.

Harwood, R. L., Miller, J. G., and Lucca Irizarry, N. *Culture and Attachment: Perceptions of the Child in Context.* New York: Guilford Press, 1995.

Imamoglu, E. O. "An Interdependence Model of Human Development." In C. Kagitcibasi (ed.), *Growth and Progress in Cross-Cultural Psychology.* Lisse, The Netherlands: Swets & Zeitlinger, 1987.

Kagitcibasi, C. *Family and Human Development Across Cultures.* Mahwah, N.J.: Erlbaum, 1996.

Kagitcibasi, C., and Sunar, D. "Family and Socialization in Turkey." In J. L. Roopnarine and D. B. Carter (eds.), *Parent-Child Socialization in Diverse Cultures.* Norwood, N.J.: Ablex, 1992.

Kongar, E. *Yüzyilda Türkiye, 2000li yillarda Türkiye'nin yapisi.* Istanbul: Remzi Kitabevi, 2001.

Leyendecker, B., Harwood, R., Comparini, L., and Yalcinkaya, A. "Socioeconomic Status, Ethnicity, and Parenting." In T. Luster and L. Okagaki (eds.), *Parenting: An Ecological Perspective.* (2nd ed.). Mahwah, N.J.: Erlbaum, 2005.

Lucca Irizarry, N., and Pacheco, A. M. "Intercultural Encounters of Puerto Rican Migrants." *Environment and Behavior, 24,* 1992, 226–238.

Pfluger-Schindlbeck, I. *Achte die Älteren, liebe die Jüngeren: Sozialisation türkisch-alevitischer Kinder im Heimatland und in der Migration.* Frankfurt am Main: Athenäums Monografien—Sozialwissenschaften, 1989.

Phalet, K., and Schönpflug, U. "Intergenerational Transmission in Turkish Immigrant Families: Parental Collectivism, Achievement Values, and Gender Differences." *Journal of Comparative Family Studies, 32,* 2001, 489–504.

Schiffauer, W. *Die Migration aus Subay—Türken in Deutschland: Eine Ethnographie.* Stuttgart, Germany: Klett-Cotta, 1991.

Schmidt-Koddenberg, A. *Akkulturation von Migrantinnen: Eine Studie zur Bedeutung sozialer Vergleichsprozesse von Türkinnen und deutschen Frauen.* Opladen, Germany: Leske+Budrich, 1989.

Sunar, D., and Fişek, G. O. "Contemporary Turkish Families." In J. L. Roopnarine and U. P. Gielen (eds.), *Families in Global Perspective.* Needham, Mass.: Allyn and Bacon, 2005.

Tobin, J. J., Wu, D.Y.H., and Davidson, D. H. *Preschool in Three Cultures.* New Haven, Conn.: Yale University Press, 1989.

U.S. Census Bureau. *The Hispanic Population: Census 2000 Brief.* 2000. Retrieved Sept. 27, 2006, from http://www.census.gov/prod/2001pubs/c2kbr01-3.pdf.

ROBIN L. HARWOOD *is a visiting professor in the Department of Psychology, Ruhr University, Bochum, Germany.*

ALEV YALÇINKAYA *is an instructor in the Department of Psychology, University of Massachusetts, Boston.*

BANU CITLAK *is a research sociologist in the Department of Psychology, Ruhr University, Bochum, Germany.*

BIRGIT LEYENDECKER *is a research psychologist in the Department of Psychology, Ruhr University, Bochum, Germany.*

NEW DIRECTIONS FOR CHILD AND ADOLESCENT DEVELOPMENT • DOI: 10.1002/cad

3

There are similarities and differences in the concept of respect as it develops in American children and adolescents whose families came from Vietnam, Cambodia, Thailand, Laos, and the Philippines. In addition, respect has different effects on adjustment, relationships, and achievement at home and at school, depending on whether cultural groups were primarily refugees or immigrants.

Respect in Southeast Asian American Children and Adolescents: Cultural and Contextual Influences

Carl L. Bankston III, Danielle Antoinette Hidalgo

People of Southeast Asian ancestry are among the newest and most rapidly growing ethnic groups in the United States. In 1970, Filipino Americans made up the only Southeast Asian national origin category with a substantial representation in this country, with a population of just over 343,000 according to U.S. Census estimates (Bankston, 2005). A 1965 change in American immigration laws helped to promote emigration from a variety of Asian nations to the United States, but the growth of populations originating from several nations of Southeast Asia resulted primarily from the end of American involvement in the war centered in Vietnam. By 1980, the numbers of Vietnamese, Cambodians, and Lao in the United States had grown from negligible to 261,729 Vietnamese, 16,044 Cambodians, and 47,683 Lao. Thailand, home to U.S. military bases during the Vietnam War, was the birthplace or ancestral homeland of 46,279 people in the United States by 1980. The Philippines was another location of U.S. military bases, which contributed to a rapidly increasing Filipino American population; it more than doubled in the 1970s, reaching 774,942 by 1980. By the end of the twentieth century, the Southeast Asian American population had grown to well over 3.5 million people, living in nearly every state in the United States.

These rapidly growing national groups constituted a new and substantial presence in American schools by the beginning of the twenty-first

NEW DIRECTIONS FOR CHILD AND ADOLESCENT DEVELOPMENT, no. 114, Winter 2006 © Wiley Periodicals, Inc.
Published online in Wiley InterScience (www.interscience.wiley.com) • DOI: 10.1002/cad.173

century. From 1980 to 2000, the students in American schools who claimed a Southeast Asian race or ancestry, from primary through college levels, grew from about 927,000 to an estimated 1.2 million. This group now represents approximately one out of every sixty-four American students. Most of the Southeast Asians (over 1 million in 2000) were enrolled in public schools. As in the population at large, the greatest numbers of Southeast Asian students were Vietnamese (112,789 in 1980 and 379,179 in 2000) and Filipinos (270,194 in 1980 and 543,327 in 2000).

American students with Southeast Asian backgrounds came from a variety of cultural traditions. The Thai, Lao, and Cambodians came from societies heavily influenced by Theravada Buddhism and by extensive historical contact with India. The Vietnamese received influences from the Mahayana Buddhism of the North and from Chinese Confucianism, as well as more recent influences from the French and Catholicism. The Philippines experienced hundreds of years of Spanish and later American colonialism. But for all of their differences, most of the immigrants from Southeast Asia came from village-based societies with cultures deeply rooted in rice farming. All of these societies emphasize age-based hierarchies and conspicuous displays of respect by younger people toward elders and people in positions of authority. As Whiting and Whiting (1975) and Whiting and Edwards (1988) argued in their cross-cultural studies of children, cultures can be seen as falling into general types, and similar types of cultures teach children to behave in similar ways.

In this chapter, we suggest that cultural traditions of respect play a large part in shaping how children and adolescents of Southeast Asian backgrounds adapt to life in American schools. We argue that while their Southeast Asian cultural traditions are different from those of most Americans, the traditions generally contribute to positive adaptation at school, although the differences may also result in some negative effects.

There are both similarities and differences running across the respective cultural values of these Southeast Asian national groups. In this chapter, we argue that these variations have less to do with differences among the core traditions of the various homelands than with distinctions in recent historical circumstances. Specifically, we propose that the ways in which Southeast Asian nationalities have expressed orientations such as age and authority hierarchies in the United States differ largely depending on whether they have arrived in the United States primarily as refugee groups or as nonrefugee immigrant groups. The distinction between immigrants as voluntary acculturating groups and refugees as involuntary acculturating groups has been widely recognized in the literature on cross-cultural adaptation (Ward, 2001; Berry and Sam, 1997).

One might at first think that the refugee groups, fleeing from war and social disruption in their homelands, would have experienced substantial disruption of their traditional cultural values and that refugee status would lead to both loss of their original homeland cultures and difficulty fitting into a host society. Indeed, the literature has generally found that refugees experience greater acculturative stress than immigrants do (Ward, 2001). However, our work in this area has led us to conclude, as we detail in this chapter, that in many cases, the refugee groups are actually more likely than the nonrefugee groups to emphasize traditional Southeast Asian cultural orientations in their interpersonal relations and that these orientations can help in adaptation to a host country. We suggest that this occurs, first, because the refugee groups often have a greater need than others to rely on intensive cooperation with coethnics, which can lead refugees to cultivate ties to other group members based on shared cultural practices and values.

By contrast, immigrants often have greater access than refugees to the opportunities and social structures of mainstream American society and have less need to rely on closed social circles of fellow immigrants for support. Second, refugees have generally arrived with national waves of population movement, while nonrefugee immigrants more often arrive in the United States as a result of individual movements, based on their individual personal connections within the larger American society. Immigration through marriage to U.S. citizens and residents, a particularly important source of migration for Southeast Asians from the nonrefugee nations of the Philippines and Thailand, is one of the most notable ways in which country-of-origin cultural connections are weakened.

Research in the schools indicates that values such as the hierarchical respect common among Southeast Asians generally benefit students who hold these values (Bankston, Caldas, and Zhou, 1997; Bankston and Zhou, 1998; Caplan, Choy, and Whitmore, 1991; Whitmore, Trautmann, and Caplan, 1989). Respect for teachers, for example, leads to cooperative behavior on the part of students and positive responses by the teachers. While nonrefugee groups often enjoy more advantageous socioeconomic positions than the refugee groups do, the socioeconomic advantages of nonrefugees tend to be counterbalanced by the advantages of the value orientations of refugees. However, as members of the refugee nationalities gradually assimilate into the broader American society over the course of generations, they may tend to lose the values that were initially positive distinctions and advantageous in U.S. schools.

Patterns of Respect in Southeast Asian Cultures

A brief examination of cultural values and practices among Southeast Asians suggests that respect occupies a key part in the value systems of all of the national groups examined here. Cultural values of respect are so deeply embedded, in fact, that these values run through the languages of Southeast Asia (Bankston and Zhou, 1998). Bankston and Zhou found that the value and practice of respect were key signifiers of Vietnamese identity and of positions in the web of Vietnamese social relations: "respect for elders and authority, as a set of collectively held ideas about desirable and undesirable forms of behavior, translates into actions that mark one's position in a hierarchy of social relations" (1998, p. 95). Respect therefore is constructed as both a cultural value and a representation of one's character and social status.

Vietnamese patterns of social organization developed around the value of respect are implicit in the Vietnamese language. Vietnamese use status pronouns that establish the relative positions of the speaker and the person addressed. First-person, second-person, and third-person pronouns vary according to these social positions. Thus, the word *ong* is both a title (*Ong Carl*—Mr. Carl; *Ong Mei*—"Mr. American," or "the American gentleman") and a second- and third-person pronoun used to indicate respect, formality, and a degree of unfamiliarity.

In the context of schools, the word *thay* ("teacher") is one of the most important Vietnamese status pronouns. As a noun, this word is usually used as part of a compound (*thay giao* or *thay hoc*—teacher), and it means both "teacher" and "master"; the latter has the sense of both "schoolmaster" and "master of a servant." Used alone, however, it is most often a pronoun that conveys the respect a student must show to a male teacher. It may be taken as an aspect of traditional Vietnamese gender relations and of the old association of teaching with masculinity; in *co giao,* the feminine equivalent of *thay giao,* the word *co* refers simply to an unmarried woman.

Cultural practices of Cambodian communities similarly rely on notions of respect to elders, authority, peers, and self. For example, the common Theravada concept of "making merit," that is, performing virtuous acts to improve one's moral and religious standing, extends to social relations. Merit making for Cambodian Buddhists denotes more than accumulating spiritual credits for good acts. Merit-making activities and correct behavior (for example, proper comportment, appropriate attire, and correct use of gendered pronouns) are viewed as upholding the order of the universe. This might even lead one to say that expression of respect is fundamental not only to Cambodian society but also to the spiritual universe of this cultural group. Thus, one's inability or refusal to follow these sociocultural guidelines is often characterized as an act against the social order, that is, as a moral transgression.

As in the other Southeast Asian languages, Khmer has a wide variety of pronouns and honorific terms, and the choice of pronouns varies depending on the social status of both the speaker and the person addressed. Terms expressing special respect are used to address Buddhist monks. For example, the English word "I" is expressed in Khmer by the word *knyom* when speaking politely to someone, *ang* when speaking to an intimate, and *knyom preah karuna* when speaking to a monk. The word *louk* is equivalent to the English "you" when speaking politely, and the word *neak* may be used in speaking to an intimate or an inferior on the social hierarchy, such as someone of a lower social class. It is significant that while Vietnamese and Lao language forms were largely undisturbed by political change in 1975, the radical Khmer Rouge attempted to obliterate all status distinctions in the language and enforce neutral equality on all speakers during the Khmer Rouge period in power, from 1975 through 1978 (Marston, 1985, 1988).

Lao culture is quite similar to that of the Thai, described just below. In fact, the language of Laos is almost identical to dialects of northeastern Thai, and even the Central Thai and Lao languages are mutually intelligible to many speakers. Like the Vietnamese, the Lao and the Thai use status pronouns. In Lao, teachers are addressed as *khuu*, a word derived from the Sanskrit *guru* that indicates high respect for teachers. Within families, age statuses are expressed through pronouns, so that, for example, older brothers are addressed as *ai* and younger brothers as *nawng*. Within Lao families, children are expected to be subordinate to parents to a much greater extent than in contemporary American families. While American children will often argue with their parents, children in Laos are expected to obey without question.

Among the nonrefugee immigrant groups, the Thai and the Filipinos, hierarchical respect is also an essential homeland cultural value. In Thailand, Theravada Buddhism predominates: nearly 90 percent of the people are Buddhist (Van Esterik, 2000). Linked to practices of Theravada Buddhism are the practices of body awareness and control closely associated with an orientation toward relations of respect for authority, elders, and one's superiors. As anthropologist Penny Van Esterik (2000) has noted, these bodily practices are "built into the socialization of Thai children. . . . Teaching children (and foreigners) to *wai* correctly and to reproduce the hand motions of classical Thai dance are lessons in transferring body-based skills." Van Esterik describes the *wai* as a "graceful Thai gesture of greeting and showing respect by placing raised palms together and bowing the head" (p. 33). Furthermore, Van Esterik describes the Thai practice of *kalatesa*, or "attention to surfaces and appearances," where postures, gestures, and talk are always related to time and place or to the social context of an interaction. Therefore, following the practice of *kalatesa*, one *wais* with far more deference to a Buddhist monk than a peer, lowering the head with palms raised to the forehead rather than the chest.

Respect directly intersects with Thai *kalatesa* in that children learn at an early age and throughout childhood that respect for teachers, parents, elders, older sisters, brothers, and friends reflects one's ability to be "Thai" in the world and reflects a child's embodied familiarity with Thai-ness, and therefore reflects the quality of a child's upbringing. Finally, elaborate status pronouns express Thai feelings toward authority, as they do among the other Southeast Asian groups. Younger siblings address the older as *pi*, and the older address the younger as *nawng*. The words *ajaan* and *kruu* are simultaneously nouns meaning "teacher," pronouns expressing a high degree of respect (especially *ajaan*), and titles placed before an individual's name.

Filipino Americans share the cultural value of respect with other Southeast Asians and display this value through behavior and physical expressions. Four widely recognized key cultural values are *utang na loob* (moral debt), *hiya* (shame), *amor proprio* (self-esteem), and *pakikisama* (getting along with others). From the Filipino perspective, children owe an eternal debt to their parents. The cultural value *hiya* requires that individuals feel ashamed when they fail to behave according to expected social roles. These social roles are often thought of in terms of family relations even when they involve people who are not actually family members. Younger people are expected to show respect for their elders at all times. When a child greets an older person such as a grandparent, the child will show respect by taking the elder's hand and bowing slightly to touch the back of the hand with the forehead.

The pattern of showing respect for elders applies to older brothers and sisters as well. Hence, older brothers and sisters must not be treated as equals but addressed as *kuya* ("big brother") and *ate* ("big sister"). Older friends are often called *kuya* or *ate*. Children call unrelated adults *tita* ("aunt") or *tito* ("uncle"). Those who do not seem to recognize or care about these types of social relations are often referred to as *walang hiya* ("shameless"), a term that expresses very strong disapproval. Direct criticism of inappropriate behavior, however, is also considered inappropriate. Indirect criticism is usually practiced. Therefore, when people violate social expectations, others will be reluctant to criticize them openly, out of fear of offending the sense of *amor proprio*. Like the Thai practice of *kalatesa*, Filipinos practice *pakikisama*, or smooth relations among people. This practice dictates that people avoid direct confrontation. In terms of the family, *pakikisama* means that individuals should always place the interests of the family and the maintenance of relations within the family first, thus considering their own interests and desires as secondary.

The similarities and variations in patterns of respect by extension apply to ideas of disrespect. Because hierarchy is so important in Southeast Asian ideas of respect, treating those who are considered in higher positions on a hierarchy as equals is a serious form of disrespect and a source of conflict within many Southeast Asian families. Women are expected to respect men, and children are expected to respect their elders. Superiors of any sort, particularly teachers for children and adolescents, must be treated with signs of respect. In the American setting, this attitude of hierarchical respect continues to be held, especially by the members of the refugee groups, who are often less accustomed than Filipino and Thai Americans to mainstream American forms of expression.

Body language easily conveys disrespect as a form of nonverbal communication. Among the Vietnamese, it is considered disrespectful and challenging to look someone in the eyes. This conflicts directly with the cultural assumption of most Americans that not looking people in the eyes is a sign of evasiveness. Failure to follow the Thai, Lao, and Cambodian practice of bowing with palms of the hands together strikes members of these groups as disrespectful, while this practice may be regarded as excessively submissive by other Americans. Among the Thai and Lao, pointing the feet at another person, or propping feet up on a chair or table expresses extreme disrespect.

NEW DIRECTIONS FOR CHILD AND ADOLESCENT DEVELOPMENT • DOI: 10.1002/cad

Variations in Historical Background

While there are many cultural similarities among Americans of various Southeast Asian origins, there are also differences in their historical backgrounds. The most notable difference is between groups that arrived as refugees and those that did not arrive as refugees.

Refugee Nationalities. U.S. military involvement in Southeast Asia produced one of the greatest government-sponsored transoceanic population movements in history. In the spring of 1975, the U.S.-supported governments of South Vietnam, Laos, and Cambodia fell to communist forces. As a result, an exodus of refugees from these three countries began. In response to the Indochinese refugee crisis, the U.S. Congress passed the most comprehensive piece of refugee legislation in U.S. history, the Refugee Act of 1980. Indochinese refugees began entering the United States in unprecedented numbers; by 2000 the number of Vietnamese in the country had grown to over 1,110,000,000, the number of Laotians to over 167,000, and the number of Cambodians to over 178,000.

Immigrant Nationalities. The two main regular immigrant (non-refugee) Southeast Asian nationalities in the United States are Filipinos and Thai. Among all the national groups discussed in this chapter, Filipinos have the longest history of contact with the United States. Large-scale Philippine-American contacts date back to 1898, when the United States intervened in the Philippine war for independence from Spain during the Spanish American War. After defeating the Spanish, the United States continued to occupy the Philippines, and U.S. troops spent several years fighting to put down the Filipino independence forces. The United States established its own government in the Philippines and introduced elements of U.S. law and public education. Although this did result in the adoption of many American political ideals, as well as the spread of the English language in the Philippines, Filipino attitudes toward parent-child and teacher-student relations continued to be dominated by notions of hierarchical respect.

Many of the Filipinos admitted to the United States were women married to American servicemen. By one estimate, about half of all the immigrants who came to the United States between 1946 and 1965 arrived as wives of U.S. military personnel (Reimers, 1985). Spouses of U.S. service personnel who had served in the Philippines continued to make up a substantial portion of the post-1965 immigration, with much of this due to the American buildup in Southeast Asia during the Vietnam War. In 1980, one out of every four married Filipino American women had a husband who had served in the U.S. military during the Vietnam War period (Ruggles and others, 2004). The United States kept its military bases until 1991, so marriage to U.S. citizens serving in the military continued to be one source of migration. Data from the 2000 U.S. Census showed that Filipinos had one of the highest rates of out-group marriage of any minority group in the nation. Most Filipino Americans in that year were married to non-Filipinos.

This was particularly marked for women. While 47.8 percent of Filipino American men were married to women of their own group, only 22.4 percent of women were married within the group. Well over half of Filipino women (57.8 percent) were married to non-Hispanic whites, as were almost one-third (31.0 percent) of Filipino men.

Following a liberalization of immigration law in 1965, the United States became much more open to professionals from Asia. Filipinos, educated in a school system modeled on that of the United States and frequently speaking fluent English, were among the most common professional immigrants to the United States. With high rates of out-group marriage, familiarity with American culture, and heavy representation in white-collar professional occupations, Filipinos have tended to fit into American society as individuals rather than as groups. Filipino migration to the United States increased rapidly in the late twentieth century, with thirty thousand to over fifty thousand people from the Philippines arriving each year during the 1980s and 1990s (Bankston, 2005).

The Thai arrived in the United States much more recently than the Filipinos. Small numbers of Thai immigrants began to arrive after the 1965 liberalization of immigration laws. Many of the early immigrants were highly skilled professionals in areas such as medicine and engineering. During the mid- to late 1960s, a larger source of immigrants came as a result of the U.S. military personnel stationed in Thailand for the war in Vietnam, Laos, and Cambodia. Marriages between U.S. soldiers and Thai women provided a large source of this wave of immigrants. According to U.S. Census data, women made up 62 percent of the Thai American population in 1980, 63 percent in 1990, and just over 60 percent in 2000. At the end of the twentieth century, the United States was home to about 111,000 people of Thai ethnicity, making them the smallest of the Southeast Asian groups.

Implications of Historical Backgrounds

The historical backgrounds of the Southeast Asian groups have important implications for the adaptation of their children to life in the United States if these backgrounds are interpreted from the segmented assimilation perspective on the children of immigrants. Basically, this perspective, associated chiefly with the work of Alejandro Portes and Min Zhou (1993), suggests that the benefits of immediate assimilation into American society depend on the segment of American society into which immigrant children assimilate. The children of middle-class, professional immigrants can assimilate into relatively advantageous settings. The children of poorer immigrants and of immigrants who have little familiarity with American society face the prospect of assimilating into some of the most disadvantaged segments in the United States. At least one of the reasons that this assimilation can be problematic is that these disadvantaged segments of American society often have ideas about respect and disrespect that conflict with middle-class American views and are not conducive to success in schools (Zhou and Bankston, 1998).

The refugee nationalities, from the segmented assimilation point of view, had both more need for reliance on cultural values such as hierarchical respect, rooted in their ethnic communities, and more access to those values. Located on the margins of American society, their chances for upward mobility depended chiefly on their abilities to do well in school and behave in ways that drew positive responses from their teachers. Generally living in close proximity to coethnics, they had access to support and direction from elders. The Thai and the Filipinos enjoyed greater access to the benefits of mainstream American society. For these two groups, then, respect was less of a key to upward mobility than it was for young members of the refugee groups.

Southeast Asian American Children, Adolescents, and Families

Throughout the 1980s, Caplan, Choy, and Whitmore pursued a major study of the children of Vietnamese, Cambodian, and Lao refugees in the United States (Caplan, Whitmore, and Choy, 1989; Caplan, Choy, and Whitmore, 1991). They were particularly interested in how cultural values brought from Southeast Asia shaped children's thinking on how life should be approached. Based on their reading of literary and historical work about the relevant nations and on reports by anthropologists and other scholars from this region, the researchers devised a questionnaire aimed at probing the central values that guide the value orientations of Southeast Asian children and their families in the United States. The researchers asked both parents and children to rate a list of items in terms of value on a five-point scale ranging from "very important" to "not at all important." Factor analyses of their results resolved the value systems into six interrelated factors: (1) the cultural foundation (connected to beliefs about religion, tradition, and society), (2) family-based achievement, (3) hard work, (4) the family in society, (5) self-reliance and pride, and (6) coping and integration. Ideas concerned with authority were prominent in three of the six clusters of values. The first element of the cultural foundation these scholars found, which was the factor that explained the greatest amount of variance in their factor analysis, was "respect for authority." "Respect for family members" was found to be one component of family-based achievement. "Respect for elders" was a key to self-reliance and pride. In a rank ordering of children's values, Caplan and his coauthors found that "respect for family members" was the single most important value of Southeast Asian children, since items reflecting this value were most often rated as "very important" or "important" by children (Caplan, Whitmore, and Choy, 1989; Choy, and Whitmore, 1991).

This value is not necessarily always passed on undisturbed to native-born generations. One of the major predictors of juvenile delinquency among young members of Southeast Asian refugee groups is the extent to which the minors reject the value of respect toward their elders. The struggle of parents with life in the new country can often lead them to lose their high-status position in the eyes of their children (for examples among the Lao, see Bankston, 2002).

Young Thai and Filipinos tend to have much looser connections to family-based values such as hierarchical respect. Cadge and Sangdhanoo (2005) report that second-generation Thai Americans show little interest in the Buddhist religion, which is at the heart of Thai culture. In terms of showing embodied or behavioral respect for elders, Filipino American children often find the practice of placing the hands of elders against their foreheads humiliating (Bankston, 2002).

Implications for Children and Adolescents in American Schools

Children in the Caplan, Whitmore, and Choy (1989) study consistently recognized "respect for family members" as their chief value when asked to list the values that were important to them. Zhou and Bankston (2000), in discussing Vietnamese children, remarked that "respect for others . . . rooted in the concept of familial hierarchy, leads children to subordinate their own immediate wishes to family goals and to accept the parental emphasis on achievement through education" (p. 48). They also noted that the children's second highest value of respect was "education and achievement," symbolizing the compatibility and connection between these two values: respect for elders and educational success.

Although concepts of hierarchical respect rooted in Southeast Asian societies are in some ways inconsistent with American egalitarianism, these concepts promote school success in American schools in at least three ways. First, the subordination of children's wishes to those of their elders places adult goals before the goals of young people. Since adults tend to focus more on the long term, this means that motivations such as immediate gratification and pleasure become secondary to school success. Second, the hierarchical ordering of social relations encourages cooperation aimed at educational achievement. Researchers have described how older siblings help younger siblings with schoolwork in families from Southeast Asian refugee groups, particularly the Vietnamese (Caplan, Choy, and Whitmore, 1991; Bankston, 1998; Rumbaut and Ima, 1988). Third, although American society in general may adhere in many ways to a consciously egalitarian ideology, American schools are conservative and hierarchical institutions. Teachers and administrators respond well to respectful treatment, and value for respect is part of the ideology of most American school systems.

It is notable that research on the three refugee groups has suggested that Cambodian youth are adjusting to American school environments much less successfully than Vietnamese and Lao youth (Kim, 2002). Among

NEW DIRECTIONS FOR CHILD AND ADOLESCENT DEVELOPMENT • DOI: 10.1002/cad

these three, the Cambodians have been the least able to maintain integrated social networks on the family or community level and pass on cultural values such as respect to younger people as a result of the social and physical devastation of their homeland in the 1970s. Cambodian parents have been described as unable to exercise much control over their children (Zhou, Bankston, and Kim, 2002). Among the Vietnamese, on average, the most academically successful of the three immigrant groups, "tight family and community social relations support beliefs about upward mobility . . . that are essential to school success" (Bankston, 2004, p. 177). Close connections to parents and other elders, fostered through respect, lead children to internalize parents' beliefs about upward mobility.

Within families, hierarchical respect creates both an obligation on the part of older siblings to help in the education of younger siblings and an obligation on the part of younger siblings to cooperate. The role of parents as authority figures, and their limited familiarity with American schools, tends to place parents in the position of establishing general expectations to be fulfilled by children. Within schools, respect for authority works well. Teachers respond well to the respect they receive from Vietnamese students, further developing positive generalizations and stereotypes of Vietnamese American students based on these experiences (Bankston, 2004).

Both Filipino and Thai young people in the United States, living in groups characterized by greater assimilation and looser ties to traditional homeland cultures than the refugee groups, have also displayed high levels of educational attainment. This has been attributed to their favorable socioeconomic positions (Bankston and Hidalgo, 2006; Bankston, 2005). It has been noted, though, that the academic performance of Filipino Americans in major subjects, as indicated by report card grades, are similar to those of whites (as one would expect of a largely assimilated group), while grades of other major Asian groups are generally significantly higher than those of whites (Bankston, 2005). There has been little research on Thai American youth in American schools, but this is precisely because there is so little that distinguishes them from other American youth. In fact, of the estimated 25,487 young people from Thai backgrounds in American schools in the year 2000, 10,047 (over 41 percent) were of mixed racial/ethnic background as a result of the high degree of marital assimilation (U.S. Census Bureau, 2000).

Conclusion

Caplan, Choy, and Whitmore (1991) concluded their book on the academic achievement of children from Vietnam, Cambodia, and Laos by observing that "the major reasons for the refugee children's success can be attributed to beliefs and family practices that, although non-Western in origin, coincide closely with traditional, mainstream, middle-class American presumptions about the values and means-ends relationships necessary for achievement" (p. 156). This chapter can be seen as a "yes, but . . ." response to that statement. In concentrating on the concept of hierarchical respect, which we argue is a central element of the value systems of Southeast Asian groups, we have maintained that this does indeed make a key contribution to academic achievement. However, although this value does fit well in certain American institutional settings such as the school, our description of Southeast Asian hierarchical values raises questions about just how much these coincide with traditional, mainstream, middle-class American presumptions. The situation may well be more ironic than these authors realize. In fact, it appears that value orientations recognizable to middle-class Americans, yet different from the orientations widely held by middle-class Americans, pay off well for Southeast Asian Americans in that most American of settings, the school.

Furthermore, the experiences of Southeast Asian children and adolescents and their parents are not simply a matter of coming from a nation with a cultural perspective that emphasizes hierarchical respect. Combining the idea of culture with that of the segmented assimilation argument, we have suggested that having this kind of non-Western value orientation is most important for those who enter it in some of its least advantaged segments and need to draw on cultural values from outside the United States to achieve mobility inside it. Furthermore, we have suggested that those who have the greatest need for hierarchical respect to achieve upward mobility in American society (for example, the Vietnamese and the Lao) are precisely the national groups most likely to have preserved it.

Differences between the refugee and immigrant Southeast Asian groups have significant implications for the psychological development and lives of their children. Filipino and Thai American children experience some intergenerational tension, but their families are frequently assimilating into relatively advantageous American settings while the children learn from peers and the larger society in those settings. Children from the three refugee groups, however, must contend with a much greater gap between their families and the surrounding European American community. At the same time, their immediate situations within American society offer refugee groups few opportunities for upward mobility. Within the home, this means that children from the refugee groups tend to either develop close ties to parents and siblings or reject their families altogether. In school, the either-or choice between home and surrounding society tends to have an ironic developmental effect. The irony is that assimilation of the value system of the school or peer group (or the hedonistic value system of American society at large) may tend to alienate children and adolescents from their families, who provide them with the value system that emphasizes respect. Vietnamese, Lao, and Cambodian children and adolescents who retain close ties to their families and to non-American cultures can often adjust better to American society in the long run than those who become alienated from their families' traditions of hierarchical respect.

As new third- and fourth-generation members of these groups appear, we can expect that differences among the groups and differences between them and other Americans will steadily diminish. Young members of all these groups, even the groups that retain the tightest grips on their cultural heritages, are already tending to adopt English as their preferred language and to take up the tastes and outlooks of other American young people.

References

Bankston, C. L. "Sibling Cooperation and Scholastic Performance Among Vietnamese-American Secondary School Students: An Ethnic Social Relations Theory." *Sociological Perspectives,* 1998, *41,* 167–184.

Bankston, C. L. "Delinquency and Diffusion: A Study of the Development of Suburban Laotian Youth Gangs." Paper presented at the annual meetings of the Southern Sociological Society, Baltimore, Md., 2002.

Bankston, C. L. "Social Capital, Cultural Values, and Academic Achievement: The Host Country Context and Contradictory Consequences." *Sociology of Education,* 2004, *77,* 176–179.

Bankston, C. L. "Filipino Americans." In P. G. Min (ed.), *Asian Americans: Contemporary Issues and Themes.* Thousand Oaks, Calif.: Pine Forge Press, 2005.

Bankston, C. L., Caldas, S. J., and Zhou, M. "The Academic Achievement of Vietnamese American Students: Ethnicity as Social Capital." *Sociological Focus,* 1997, *30,* 1–16.

Bankston, C. L., and Hidalgo, D. A. "Southeast Asia: Laos, Cambodia, and Thailand." In M. Waters and R. Ueda (eds.), *The New Americans: A Guide to Immigration Since 1965.* Cambridge, Mass.: Harvard University Press, 2006.

Bankston, C. L., and Zhou, M. *Growing up American: How Vietnamese Children Adapt to Life in the U.S.* New York: Russell Sage Foundation, 1998.

Berry, J. W., and Sam, D. "Acculturation and Adaptation." In J. W. Berry, M. H. Segall, and C. Kagitcibasi (eds.), *Handbook of Cross-Cultural Psychology.* Vol. 3: *Social Behavior and Applications.* Needham Heights, Mass.: Allyn and Bacon, 1997.

Cadge, W., and Sangdhanoo, S. "Thai Buddhism in America: A Historical and Contemporary Overview." *Contemporary Buddhism,* 2005, *6,* 7–35.

Caplan, N. H., Choy, M. H., and Whitmore, J. K. *Children of the Boat People: A Study of Educational Success.* Ann Arbor: University of Michigan Press, 1991.

Caplan, N. H., Whitmore, J. K., and Choy, M. H. *The Boat People and Achievement in America: A Study of Economic and Educational Success.* Ann Arbor: University of Michigan Press, 1989.

Kim, R. Y. "Ethnic Differences in Academic Achievement Between Vietnamese and Cambodian Children." *Sociological Quarterly,* 2002, *43,* 213–235.

Marston, J. "Language Reform in Democratic Kampuchea." Paper presented at the Minnesota Regional Conference on Linguistics and the Philosophy of Language, Minneapolis, Minn., 1985.

Marston, J. "Language Use and Language Policy in Democratic Kampuchea." Paper presented at the Colloquium on Language Use and Language Policy in Laos, Cambodia, and Vietnam, University of Hawaii at Manoa, 1988.

Portes, A., and Zhou, M. "The New Second Generation: Segmented Assimilation and Its Variants Among Post-1965 Immigrant Youth." *Annals of the American Academy of Political and Social Science,* 1993, *530,* 74–98.

Reimers, D. M. *Still the Golden Door: The Third World Comes to America.* New York: Columbia University Press, 1985.

Ruggles, S., and others. *Integrated Public Use Microdata Series (Version 3.0).* Minneapolis: Minnesota Population Center, 2004. Machine-readable database.

Rumbaut, R., and Ima, K. *The Adaptation of Southeast Asian Refugee Youth: A Comparative Study.* Washington, D.C.: U.S. Office of Refugee Resettlement, 1988.

U.S. Census Bureau. *U.S. Census 2000, Summary File 4*. Washington, D.C.: Government Printing Office, 2000.

Van Esterik, M. *Materializing Thailand*. Oxford: Berg Press, 2000.

Ward, C. "The A,B,Cs of Acculturation." In D. Matsumoto (ed.), *The Handbook of Cultural Psychology*. New York: Oxford University Press, 2001.

Whiting, B. B., and Edwards, C. P. *Children of Different Worlds: The Formation of Social Behavior*. Cambridge, Mass.: Harvard University Press, 1988.

Whiting, B. B., and Whiting, J.W.M. *Children of Six Cultures: A Psycho-Cultural Analysis*. Cambridge, Mass.: Harvard University Press, 1975.

Whitmore, J. K., Trautmann, M., and Caplan, N. H. "The Socio-Cultural Basis for Economic and Educational Success of Southeast Asian Refugees (1978–1982 Arrivals)." In D. Haines (ed.), *Refugees as Immigrants*. Lanham, Md.: Rowman and Littlefield, 1989.

Zhou, M., and Bankston III, C. L. *Growing up American: How Vietnamese Children Adapt to Life in the United States*. New York: Russell Sage Foundation, 1998.

Zhou, M., and Bankston III, C. L. *Straddling Two Social Worlds: The Experience of Vietnamese Refugee Children in the U.S.* New York: Institute for Urban and Minority Education, 2000.

Zhou, M., Bankston III, C. L., and Kim, R. Y. "Rebuilding Spiritual Lives in the New Land: Religious Practices Among Southeast Asian Refugees in the U.S." In P. G. Min and J. H. Kim (eds.), *Religions in Asian America: Building Faith Communities*. Walnut Creek, Calif.: Altamira Press, 2002.

CARL L. BANKSTON III *is professor and chair of the Department of Sociology and co-director of the Asian Studies Program, Tulane University, New Orleans, Louisiana.*

DANIELLE ANTOINETTE HIDALGO *is a doctoral candidate in the Department of Sociology, University of California, Santa Barbara.*

NEW DIRECTIONS FOR CHILD AND ADOLESCENT DEVELOPMENT • DOI: 10.1002/cad

The meaning of respect changed historically in postwar Japan, and respect as a concept is important yet unnoticed in postmodern Japanese society. Contrary to the perception of Japanese socialization as instilling conformist respect and obedience in children and adolescents, this chapter shows why one commentator predicts that Japan may be changing from a "society of respect" to a "society of scorn."

Respect in Japanese Childhood, Adolescence, and Society

Shuji Sugie, David W. Shwalb, Barbara J. Shwalb

Respect as a social attitude transcends culture, but when we apply the term *respect* there are various cultural differences in the meaning of the word. In this chapter we consider how respect is understood in Japan, and several influences on respectful behavior and understanding of respect. Citing the results of research studies and based on our interpretation of psychological, linguistic, historical, and societal factors, we will demonstrate two contrasting trends: (1) a historical change of some aspects of Japanese-style respect, and (2) cultural continuities that have made respect central to Japanese human development and human relations. We bring together here the viewpoints of both a native of Japan (Sugie) and that of Americans who have lived long term in Japan (Shwalbs).

We examine respect as manifested in childhood and adolescence, in relation to survey research data and issues specific to Japanese families, schools, and communities. In Japanese culture, there is a strong degree of conformity and little tolerance for uncertainty. Accordingly, interpersonal relationships are based on a sense of security and predictability in daily life. These tendencies coexist with a degree of looseness and lack of strictness in personal relations, resulting in two types of respect in Japanese culture. In the first form of respect, the greatest amount of respect is paid to one's parents and may be understood as related to affection in a close attachment relationship. A second type of respect is found in more distal personal relations, where there is a status difference between individuals. When this latter type of respect is shown in formal settings, one's status is expressed in

NEW DIRECTIONS FOR CHILD AND ADOLESCENT DEVELOPMENT, no. 114, Winter 2006 © Wiley Periodicals, Inc.
Published online in Wiley InterScience (www.interscience.wiley.com) • DOI: 10.1002/cad.174

a ceremonious respectful manner (*tatemae*) but may not correspond to one's true feelings (*honne*). We will see that this form of respect has weakened in Japanese culture in recent years and that respect in distal and formal relationships is undergoing a particularly rapid transformation.

Background

To understand the nature of respect in contemporary Japanese childhood and adolescence, we must first recognize that childhood, adolescence, and Japanese culture itself have changed historically and continue to change (Hara and Minagawa, 1996).

Defining *Respect*. A popular Japanese dictionary defines *respect* as "cognizant of the extraordinary aspects of a person's achievements and conduct, and looking up to a person as a desirable model" (Yamada, Shibata, Sakai, and Kuramochi, 2005, p. 875). An earlier source had defined *respect* as "acknowledging the strong points of a person's character or behavior, and feeling the desire to bow down to or follow after a person" (Nishio, Iwabuchi, and Mizutani, 1983, p. 650). Both definitions suggest that respect has behavioral, cognitive, and affective aspects regarding another person who is in some way better than oneself. However, there is one important difference between the two definitions. Yamada, Shibata, Sakai, and Kuramochi emphasized achievements and conduct as attributes of the target person, whereas Nishio, Iwabuchi, and Mizutani's definition also included an evaluation of another's attributes of the person. As expressions of reverence or desire to be a follower, respect in the latter view would clearly affect the nature of relations between the giver and recipient of respect. The idea of being a follower has a connotation of subordination and dependency, but respect in Nishio, Iwabuchi, and Mizutani's view was not equated with identification or emulation.

Lack of Public and Scholarly Attention to Respect. When the Japanese Ministry of Education, Culture, Sports, Science and Technology determines the fundamental direction of national educational policies, its Central Council for Education (made up of scholars) has an important role in making recommendations to the ministry. The council's 1996 report, *A Model for Japanese Education in the Perspective of the 21st Century*, did not mention the word *respect* a single time. As Li and Yokoyama (2000a) observed, "Due to various circumstances in the postwar era the word 'respect' has been made light of or ignored. Nowadays children's awareness of respect toward historical figures, or the elderly, parents, and teachers, whom one might traditionally have looked up to, has weakened considerably" (p. 227).

There has been remarkably little psychological research on respect in Japan. A search of the indexes of several representative Japanese psychology dictionaries and handbooks for the term *respect* revealed no citations (Nakajima and others, 1999; Azuma, Shigeta, and Tajima, 1992; Kuze and Saito, 2000). Neither was there any reference to respect in a dictionary of sociology (Mita, Kurihara, and Tanaka, 1988). Further, a search of journal articles in the holdings of the Japanese National Diet Library since 1995 revealed only three empirical studies of respect, in addition to several commentaries and a few public surveys, which we review in the following section.

Awareness of Respect in Japanese Childhood and Adolescence

Some non-Japanese observers of Japanese culture give the impression that Japanese school children and adolescents are well behaved and respectful of their teachers. However, research evidence provides a more complex alternative view of respect in middle childhood and adolescence in school settings.

School Children. Li and Yokoyama's (2002a) questionnaire survey about the awareness of respect among Japanese sixth-grade children found the following:

- Over 90 percent of children understood the meaning of the word *respect*.
- Children tended to view respect as a desire to be like someone else, that is, "identification."
- Over 90 percent of children thought of respect as a good thing.
- Only 40 percent had been taught to respect those who are of higher status or older than themselves.
- As to attributes of a respectable person, children most often mentioned people who were gentle, courteous, or superior in ability and seldom mentioned people of wealth or fame.
- Common recipients of respect were people who were in one's family or other blood relations.
- About 75 percent of children wanted to be like the people they respected, and 90 percent liked them.

These findings revealed that Japanese school children were aware of respect, yet a majority had little experience at school and home related to respect. They also tended to respect people with whom they were close, suggesting that respect was related to their feelings of attachment.

Li and Yokoyama (2000b) compared the preceding data with data from a sample of Chinese elementary school children. China and Japan both have a legacy of reverence and respect for the elderly based on Confucianism. However, there were several differences in children's understanding of respect between the two cultural samples:

- Although children in both cultures recognized the value of respect, Chinese children had a greater tendency to want to be respected by others.
- Chinese children had stronger respect for people who were older or of higher status.

NEW DIRECTIONS FOR CHILD AND ADOLESCENT DEVELOPMENT • DOI: 10.1002/cad

- Almost 100 percent of Chinese children had been educated to show respect.
- As to what kinds of people were worthy of respect, Chinese children emphasized gentle, older, and knowledgeable people.
- More Chinese listed grandparents than parents as deserving of respect, and more Chinese than Japanese children listed their teachers as worthy of respect.

In contrast with the Japanese sample, Chinese children in the comparison seemed to respect older and high-status individuals unconditionally and were more likely to have some training to show respect.

Middle School and High School Students. The Japan Youth Research Institute (2000) compared samples of fifteen- to eighteen-year old adolescents in the United States, China, and Japan. Table 4.1 presents comparative middle school data about respect for one's father, mother, teacher, and friends. The overall responses of high school students in the three societies were quite similar. The data also showed that Chinese middle school students were more likely than their Japanese or American peers to list parents and teachers as recipients of respect. In addition, fewer Japanese youth than American youth reported that parents and teachers were worthy of respect.

In addition, the Japanese data differed from Chinese responses in that fewer Japanese adolescents agreed that different people "must be obeyed." In this sense, the Japanese responses were somewhat similar to those of American middle school students. About half of the Japanese students agreed with the statement that they had a superficial relationship with their teachers, which was a higher proportion than in the American or Chinese samples. In contrast with their relationship with parents, with whom they

Table 4.1. Comparison of Japanese, American, and Chinese Middle School Students

		Japan	United States	China
This person must be respected:	Father	31.0%	46.5%	72.8%
	Mother	26.9	51.4	71.8
	Teacher	12.8	25.8	79.5
	Friend	20.8	24.4	25.9
This person must be obeyed:	Father	36.2	39.5	67.8
	Mother	24.7	26.4	70.6
	Teacher	24.4	24.6	54.1
	Friend	5.8	10.8	4.9
I relate to this person in a superficial way:	Father	6.1	14.9	8.0
	Mother	6.3	15.6	2.5
	Teacher	48.8	19.6	27.6
	Friend	28.3	22.6	22.6

Source: Japan Youth Research Institute (2000).

NEW DIRECTIONS FOR CHILD AND ADOLESCENT DEVELOPMENT • DOI: 10.1002/cad

felt close, Japanese students observed a degree of superficiality rather than respect toward authority figures. This is illustrated by the proverb, "*Shi no kage wa nana shaku sagatte fumazu,*" which means that teachers are worthy of so much deference that one should pass at a distance of about two meters from them to avoid stepping even on their shadows. These findings and the data of Li and Yokoyama (2002a) suggest that relationships in Japanese childhood and adolescence are seldom based on respect. A more recent study (Benesse Educational Research and Development Center, 2006) indicated, as shown in Table 4.2, that Japanese parents of preschoolers emphasized kindness over being respected as goals for their children more than did samples of parents in China and Taiwan.

The Sociocultural Context of Respect in Japan

Japanese children and youth understand and express respect in the context of societal values, norms of interpersonal behavior based on dependency and status differentiation, historical changes in the Japanese emperor system, and changes in the use of honorific speech.

Japanese Respect in Relation to Interpersonal Trust. Despite individual differences in personality, Japan has often been described as a relatively collectivistic culture (Hamaguchi and Kumon, 1982). If this generalization is true, Japanese would tend to be skillful at living securely within groups and be adept in deepening of interpersonal relations. However, psychological research has shown that Japanese interpersonal relations are sometimes superficial, which makes it difficult to establish deep connections with others. This was seen in Yamagishi and Yamagishi's comparative study (1994) of American and Japanese attitudes about trust, in which participants were asked whether they agreed with the following statements:

• Most people are fundamentally honest.
• Most people are reliable.
• Most people are basically kind and forthright.

Table 4.2. Comparison of Parents' Views of Preschoolers in Japan, China, and Taiwan

	Tokyo	Seoul	Beijing	Shanghai	Taipei
I hope that in the future my child will be . . .					
Respected by others	12.0%	28.3%	45.5%	43.0%	23.2%
Kind to others	74.5	14.3	14.2	11.3	13.9
A leader	6.1	46.8	15.5	25.6	22.4

Source: Benesse Educational Research and Development Center (2006).

- Most people trust each other.
- I tend to trust people.
- Most people, when they are trusted, trust others.

In response to these six items, male and female college students and adults in Japan reported less feelings of trust in others compared with their American counterparts. Some Japanese people, if we may generalize from these data, may lack a feeling of trust in others. Yamagishi (1998, 1999) also noted that trust requires a person to overcome social uncertainty in personal relationships and that in the Japanese context of a relatively homogeneous population, it is possible to get along without evaluating the other person. Yamagishi and others (1995) concluded that in a culture with weakness in the form of social uncertainty (an inability to predict the social behavior of others), it is difficult to make interpersonal commitments. As a result, respect causes stress when it requires one to pass judgment on the recipient of respect. The person who receives respect also experiences stress under the pressure to behave in a respectable manner. These social psychological findings provide one reason that it can be difficult for people in contemporary Japan to give and receive respect.

Respect and the Japanese Imperial System. From the time of the Meiji Restoration of 1868, when Japan opened itself up to the Western world, through the end of World War II in 1945, Japan had an imperial government, and the educational system was based on decrees that required absolute obedience toward the emperor and nation. Following the defeat of Japan in World War II, reforms swept away the prewar educational system, eliminating most objects of previous loyalty and devotion. This was a major cause of the decline in the importance of respect that has taken place in Japan over the past sixty years. In the postwar era, the emperor continued to be the symbol of the country, but longitudinal data have shown a change in public sentiment toward the emperor. For example, the NHK Broadcasting Culture Research Institute (2004) in its ongoing surveys gave four choices in a question about people's feelings about the emperor: "respect," "like," "no feelings," and "feeling of opposition." NHK compared the attitudes of individuals who were born after the war with those who had experience with the war or were educated during the war. The results of this survey are shown in Table 4.3. The survey, which was conducted every five years from 1973 through 2003, revealed a significant shift in public sentiment between 1988 and 1993. From 1973 to 1988, the findings were stable, and they stabilized again between 1993 and 2003.

The reason for these shifts in public sentiment clearly was that the Showa emperor, who reigned from 1926 and throughout World War II, died in 1989. People who lived from before the war were imbued with a fixed sense of respect for the emperor that they could not easily change. However, when the Showa emperor's son, who had been viewed by the Japanese since his childhood as a prince, became emperor, feelings toward him were mainly based on liking and attachment. Thus, the prototypical object of respect in

Table 4.3. Historical Changes in Respect for the Japanese Emperor

	Year of Survey	Respect	Like	No Feelings	Feelings of Opposition	No Response
Prewar born or	1988	52%	24%	21%	1%	2%
wartime educated	1993	42	41	14	1	3
Postwar born	1988	17	24	55	2	2
	1993	12	50	35	1	1

Source: NHK Broadcasting Culture Research Institute (2004).

Japan lost its place. The postwar generation had not experienced prewar education and had a strong feeling of separation from the imperial system. However, because the new emperor became a familiar figure to the public through the mass media and did nothing objectionable, he became more "likable" than respectable.

Society forced on the Japanese people a "reverent" formal type of respect between the Meiji era and defeat in World War II. We do not believe that authority-based respect was rooted in the culture itself. Although the emperor was a special subject, when his authority was no longer based on coercion, the Japanese reverted to their weak sense of uncertainty, and their relationship to the emperor became based on liking and attachment. This may have resulted in a gradual change in the Japanese dictionary definition of *respect*, shown, for example, by Yamada's exclusion (2005) of subordination as part of respect. As noted previously, many Japanese children appear to have respect for their parents because they are close to them. It is reasonable to conclude that in Japan, respect probably includes a strong element of attachment and that the more formal type of respect is in decline.

Honorific Language. In Japanese, the type of language used in speaking with someone who is of higher status than oneself is called *keigo*, or honorific speech. The complexity of this language is one of the reasons it is difficult for non-natives to master the Japanese language. This is true not only for us (Shwalb co-authors), for whom Japanese is our second language, but honorific speech is indeed increasingly difficult to teach to native Japanese children and is used less in succeeding generations of Japanese adolescents. There are three types of honorific speech: respect language (*sonkeigo*), modest/humble language (*kenjohgo*), and polite language (*teineigo*). Of these three, respect language expresses respect for the other person. For example, when we give a gift to a person of higher status, we say *sashi-ageru*, and we raise the object above our heads in the gesture of handing the gift to the other person. Modest/humble language signifies that one is lower in status than the other person, and we use an expression to elevate the relative status of that person. When we receive a gift within this status relationship, we say *itadaku* and

lower our head in a bow of humility. Finally, in polite language, we are especially careful to show the other person that we treat that person as important.
    There has been a tendency to move away from the use of honorific
speech, which has a long history of use in Japan. The main reason for this
is that many families no longer teach honorific language as part of child-
rearing. Yet in modern egalitarian Japanese society, a formal style of mutual
interaction is necessary, and this might be one reason that honorific language
persists in postmodern Japan. There may often be occasions when the honorific is the proper form of behavior but the person does not really experience
the emotion of respect. In this situation, we have distal or ceremonial respect.
Ceremonial behavior may differ from one's true feelings, but if it is not com-
pelled it is inevitable that such proper behavior will gradually disappear.
    Public Behavior Versus Private Feelings.   In Japanese, *honne* refers to
one's true inner feelings, whereas *tatemae* is the outward behavior revealed in
public. In an egalitarian society, one might express a formal style of *tatemae*,
for example, in following the rules for where to sit at a meal. Respect language
is used in a ceremonial sense to avoid conflict between people of different statuses, and this type of communication became natural and normal in Japanese. It would be an exaggeration to say that young people learn simply to
disguise their feelings of disrespect (*honne*) with displays of respect (*tatemae*).
But the *tatemae/honne* duality is relevant to the duality of respect and disrespect
in some situations. An interesting subject for future research would be to examine how children and adolescents learn to express and understand *tatemae* and
honne in communication between people of different statuses. We believe that
there is a trend in Japan away from the socialization of children and adolescents to understand the distinction between public principles and private feelings, and that this trend is related to the decline in teaching of formal respect.
    Respect and Human Relations of Dependency.   Doi (1973) indicated
that *amae* (sometimes roughly translated as dependency) is at the core of
interpersonal relations among the Japanese. The word *amae* is derived from
the word *amai*, which means "sweet tasting." In the Japanese cultural context,
it is a personal approach in which one may anticipate that other people will
not respond harshly. It is also expected that we would not back another person into a corner, and even if there were an interpersonal problem, we should
behave in a way that is mutually accepting and tolerant. But even with the
spread of *amae* in daily life, society was set up in a way that would not permit
the *amae* of the imperial system until the time of defeat in World War II. The
institution of the family in wartime Japan emphasized the leadership of
the paternal line, but with the defeat of Japan, this framework was demolished.
With the formal democratization of Japanese society, people did not move
from vertical relationships toward individualism, and instead reverted to a culture of *amae*. A period of great economic expansion and changes in lifestyle
occurred in the 1960s, which complicated human relations even more.
    The legacy of Japanese-style Confucian ethics is based on the benign
protection from the superior person. This gives the higher-status person

great responsibility. If one does not take this responsibility, personal relationships do not function well, especially if the lower-status person does not take the higher-status person's responsibility seriously. Based on human relations of dependency, even if we do not understand the other person clearly, we can get along with one another through mutual forgiveness and tolerance. Overall, the dependency-oriented interpersonal relations of *amae* culture may foster the development of emotion-based proximal respect rather than authority-based distal respect.

Respect in the Context of Japanese Schools

We have indicated that respect has evolved in relation to the behavioral norms, values, language, and history of Japanese society. As such, we consider respect to be a dynamic phenomenon that will continue to evolve as individuals and society change. We believe that the contexts of the family system and educational system are the two primary locations in which the development of respect takes place. Respect and disrespect may be most noticeable in public educational settings, because formal respect was once a fundamental goal of Japanese education. Therefore, commentary about the origins of respect in Japan has often focused on children's and adolescents' experiences and relationships at school. Research in this area has been concerned with respect for teachers, peers, and schools. It will be very important in future research to focus more attention on the socialization of respect and disrespect in family contexts, which has been entirely lacking in past research.

Current Conditions of Japanese Teachers. Despite research evidence indicating that Japanese school teachers are well trained and generally competent, achievement of Japanese students in international comparisons is at a very high level, and school refusal and delinquency occur at a low frequency in Japan relative to other modern nations, Japanese teachers currently do not receive a positive evaluation from the public. In the midst of recent educational reforms, teachers have been overtaken by a variety of sudden changes and are extremely busy (Fujita, 2005; Kariya, 2002). There is a trend toward increasing stress among school teachers (Itoh, 2002). Each year the number of teachers who develop psychiatric disorders is increasing, and according to a report from the Ministry of Education, Culture, Sports, Science and Technology, it tripled in 2005 from ten years ago to 0.4 percent of all teachers. In absolute terms, this is a small incidence, but the rapid increase in the percentage is significant. In addition, because class sizes in elementary, middle, and high school classrooms average about forty students, teachers work under challenging conditions. These tendencies have a bearing on the respect now accorded to school teachers by students, parents, and the general public.

Delinquency, school refusal, and bullying exist in Japanese schools, and a growing problem among students is that they have lost their sense of normative behavior (Hosaka, 2005). There has been a gradual increase overall in all of these forms of problem behavior. Many of these problems can be traced to the decline in authority within families. In spite of this, teachers are often described by the mass media and by commentators as lacking in the ability to provide guidance to students, and there is less questioning of the family's responsibility. We view this as a case of projecting the *amae* of society and the family, including permissiveness, by blaming teachers and the general school system for the problems of children and adolescents.

From an American's point of view (Shwalb co-authors), the image of Japanese teachers changed dramatically since the time of our participation in the Japanese educational system (in the mid-1970s, early 1980s, and mid-1990s). It was impressive to us then how children and adolescents seemed to accord a great degree of respect to teachers and administrators. We observed and experienced such respect in the use of the word *sensei*, standing at attention at the beginning and end of class, relatively minor difficulties with classroom management, quality training of teachers, and highly selective competition for jobs as school teachers. This positive view of the Japanese teachers and teaching may have been biased to some degree by our contrasts with the chronic problems we had witnessed in the American educational system. This suggests that the actual respect or disrespect Japanese teachers encounter might be better understood in cross-cultural perspective.

Students' Evaluation of Teachers. There has been a decline in the value of academic subject studies at school, which both students and their parents have associated with teachers' lack of guidance. Another general trend has been toward a view of teachers as gentle, a humanistic approach to student-teacher relationships, and teachers' emphasis on seeking receptiveness (Benesse Educational Research Institute, 1996). Based on Japanese *amae*-centered human relations, teachers avoid strictness and do not seek to gain the respect of students. According to other data from elementary schools, 76 percent of teachers agreed that children's respectful attitude toward teachers and other adults had declined in the past 10 years (Benesse Educational Research Institute, 1999a).

As bi-cultural educators, we realize that teaching techniques and the quality of teacher-child relationships must be understood in a cultural context. For example, in some settings, a humanistic teacher-child relationship and gentle teacher might be highly desirable. We (Shwalb co-authors) recall that our own children, when they attended public schools in Tokyo and Nagoya for several years, greatly benefited from their teachers' humanistic and child-centered approach that emphasized receptiveness to and acceptance of children. Unfortunately, another study found that the percentage of middle school teachers who agreed that "students make fools out of the teachers" was 48.7 percent (Benesse Educational Research Institute, 1999b).

Respect for Teachers and Education. Relations between students and teachers become increasingly mutual and reciprocal with age and must be based on a mutual trust. Strained relations based on ceremonial respect and dependency, under conditions of weak social uncertainty, may have the unfortunate effect of bringing about half-hearted and superficial classroom relationships. When students absorb teachers' one-sided transmission of knowledge passively and have to tolerate teachers they cannot understand, they lose awareness of what they are studying. In our opinion, there may also be a tendency among some Japanese teachers to seek popularity rather than respect from students, which may result in a decline in value of learning and lower academic achievement.

Evaluation of Public Education. According to a study by the Japanese Government Cabinet Office (2005), the level of satisfaction of parents with their children's middle and high schools is low, as follows: very satisfied, 0.3 percent; satisfied, 10.7 percent;, neither, 48.4 percent; not satisfied, 32.1 percent; and very dissatisfied, 8.5 percent. In addition, when the survey asked parents whether schools or after-school academies like *juku* or *yobiko* contribute more to adolescents' academic achievements, parents of middle school students responded in a way that reflected poorly on schools (see Table 4.4). Parents evaluated schools at a low level as far as fixing the credit for academic achievement (Shwalb, Sugie, and Yang, 2005).

Studies of adolescents' evaluations of schools also have revealed a negative view. Tomoeda and Suzuki (2003) gave eleventh-grade students (age seventeen) the statement, "I don't understand the usefulness of what we study in school," and obtained these responses: agree, 35.1 percent; agree somewhat. 35.1 percent; disagree somewhat, 19.3 percent; and disagree, 10.5 percent.

Research on how Japanese think about respect provides us with a window of understanding for broader Japanese culture. In December 2005, the Ministry of Education, Culture, Sports, Science and Technology published a document titled *Building Compulsory Education for a New Era*, and mentioned respect only six times. Of these six references, five concerned the need for teachers to cultivate respect from students, and the sixth concerned respect for one's country. This report looked at respect only in terms of training children to respect teachers in a formal ceremonial manner. It did not deal with people's real feelings about respect, self-respect, or respect for peers, which we assume would be important issues given the growing incidence of peer group problems. We wonder if this limited view of respect, as restricted to formal distal relationships, actually aggravates the problem of

Table 4.4. Parental Evaluations of the Relative Impact of Schools, *Juku*, and *Yobiko* on Academic Achievement

"Which institution contributes more to positive academic achievements?"	Schools Are Superior	Schools Do Somewhat More	Neither Does More	Juku and Yobiko Do Somewhat More	Juku and Yobiko Are Superior
Middle school	0.4%	3.7%	21.8%	40.8%	32.6%
High school	1.6	3.1	23.0	42.6	29.7

fostering attachment-based interpersonal respect in proximal relationships among Japanese children and adolescents.

Disrespect: An Emerging Problem for Child and Adolescent Development

This chapter has made little mention of disrespect, which we consider to be different from a lack of or decline in respect. There is no word in Japanese that equates directly with *disrespect,* and even fewer reference citations are available about disrespect than respect in Japanese. The words *scorn* (*kei-betsu*) and *contempt* (*bubetsu*) are more common in contrast with *respect* in Japanese than is *disrespect,* and respect and disrespect appear to be independent concepts in the Japanese language. Hayamizu (2006) wrote recently that feelings of scorn have become increasingly common among Japanese, as evidenced by his interviews with teachers at schools. Hayamizu learned from teachers that the expression of anger had increased in children over the past twenty to thirty years, while expressions of emotions, including sadness, joy, fear, and surprise, have decreased in frequency. He noted that growing numbers of Japanese children and adolescents feel better about themselves by making light of others and described Japan as in transition from a "society of respect" to a "society of scorn." We do not believe that any culture can be categorized or understood in terms of one or two words, but as educators and parents, we are concerned with the possibility of the transition that Hayamizu envisioned. It is our hope that the issues of respect and disrespect will gain more attention from Japanese educators, parents, and policymakers. In addition, cross-cultural research on respect, disrespect, and emotions such as scorn and contempt might reveal whether this ominous transition has already occurred or is happening among children and adolescents in other societies, at what ages it occurs, and whether it is preventable or reversible.

Conclusion

We have shown that respect is important to social development in Japanese childhood and adolescence and that behavioral, cognitive, and affective aspects of respect in Japan are a product of dynamic change in historical, linguistic, institutional, and societal factors. Respect takes on particular characteristics in Japan based on the blend of experiences, institutional settings, family structures, social conditions, norms, values, and historical trends to which Japanese children and adolescents are exposed. Since culture is not monolithic, individuals in every culture develop their own unique expressions of respect based on their unique set of experiences and relationships. Even the limited data reviewed here indicate that the view of Japanese as particularly respectful because of collectivistic or conformist tendencies is an outdated stereotype. An alternative view suggests a possible decline of respect and outbreak of disrespect resulting from historical changes in societal values and personal relationships in schools and families. Objective research that uses a variety of methodologies is necessary to prove which of these two views of respect in Japan is more accurate. Because we believe that respect and disrespect develop throughout childhood and adolescence, we recommend a developmental approach in such research. The implications of becoming a society of scorn or disrespect are immense for the future of Japanese children and also for intergenerational and intercultural human development and relationships.

References

Azuma, H., Shigeta, S., and Tajima, N. (eds.). *Handbook of Developmental Psychology.* Tokyo: Fukumura Shuppan, 1992. (in Japanese)

Benesse Educational Research Institute. *Students and Homeroom Teachers. The World of Middle School Students,* no. 53. Tokyo: Benesse Educational Research and Development Center, 1996. (in Japanese)

Benesse Educational Research Institute. *How Shall We Grasp the Roughness of Classrooms? Elementary School Pupils Now,* no. 19–2. Tokyo: Benesse Educational Research and Development Center, 1999a. (in Japanese)

Benesse Educational Research Institute. *Thoughts on the Roughness of Classrooms. The World of Middle School Students,* no. 53. Tokyo: Benesse Educational Research and Development Center, 1999b. (in Japanese)

Benesse Educational Research and Development Center. *A Survey About Children's Lives.* Tokyo: Benesse Educational Research and Development Center, 2006. (in Japanese)

Doi, T. *The Anatomy of Dependence.* (J. Bestor, Trans.). Tokyo: Kodansha International, 1973.

Fujita, H. *Requestioning Compulsory Education.* Tokyo: Chikuma Shobo, 2005. (in Japanese)

Hamaguchi, E., and Kumon, S. (eds.). *Japanese-Style Collectivism: Questioning Its Real Value.* Tokyo: Yuhikaku, 1982. (in Japanese)

Hara, H., and Minagawa, M. "From Productive Dependents to Precocious Guests: Historical Changes in Japanese Children." In D. Shwalb and B. Shwalb (eds.), *Japanese Childrearing: Two Generations of Scholarship.* New York: Guilford Press, 1996.

Hayamizu, T. *Youth Who Look Down on Others.* Tokyo: Kodansha, 2006. (in Japanese)

Hosaka, T. "School Absenteeism, Bullying, and Loss of Peer Relationships in Japanese Children." In D. Shwalb, J. Nakazawa, and B. Shwalb (eds.), *Applied Developmental Psychology: Theory, Practice, and Research from Japan.* Greenwich, Conn.: Information Age Publishing, 2005.

Itoh, M. *The Work of School Counselors.* Tokyo: Iwanami Shoten, 2002. (in Japanese)

Japan Youth Research Institute. *A Survey on Everyday Life.* Tokyo: Japan Youth Research Institute, 2000. (in Japanese)

Japanese Government Cabinet Office. *Results of a Survey of Parents Concerning the Educational System.* Tokyo: Japanese Government Cabinet Office, 2005. (in Japanese)

Kariya, T. *The Fantasy of Educational Reform.* Tokyo: Chikuma Shobo, 2002. (in Japanese)

Kuze, T., and Saito, K. (eds.). *Dictionary of Adolescent Psychology.* Tokyo: Fukumura Shuppan, 2000. (in Japanese)

Li, Z., and Yokoyama, M. "A Study on Concept of Attitude of Respect of Japanese Elementary School Children." *Bulletin of Fukuoka University of Education,* 2002a, *51,* 227–236. (in Japanese)

Li, Z., and Yokoyama, M. "The Comparison of Respect-Consciousness of Children in Japan and China." *Bulletin of Research Center for Teaching Practice,* 2002b, *10,* 113–120. (in Japanese)

Ministry of Education, Culture, Sports, Science, and Technology. *A Model for Japanese Education in the Perspective of the 21st Century.* Tokyo: Ministry of Education, Culture, Sports, Science, and Technology, 1996. (in Japanese)

Ministry of Education, Culture, Sports, Science, and Technology. *Building Compulsory Education for a New Era.* Tokyo: Ministry of Education, Culture, Sports, Science, and Technology, 2005. (in Japanese)

Mita, M., Kurihara, A., and Tanaka, Y. (eds.). *Dictionary of Sociology.* Tokyo: Kobundo, 1988. (in Japanese)

Nakajima, Y., and others. *Psychology Dictionary.* Tokyo: Yuhikaku, 1999. (in Japanese)

NHK Broadcasting Culture Research Institute. *The Structure of Consciousness of Contemporary Japanese.* (6th ed.) Tokyo: Nihon Hososhuppan Kyokai, 2004. (in Japanese)

Nishio, M., Iwabuchi, E., and Mizutani, S. *Iwanami Japanese Dictionary.* (3rd ed.) Tokyo: Iwanami Shoten, 1983. (in Japanese)

Shwalb, D. W., Sugie, S., and Yang, C. M. "Motivation for Abacus Studies and School Mathematics: A Longitudinal Study of Japanese 3rd to 6th Graders." In D. Shwalb, J. Nakazawa, and B. Shwalb (eds.), *Applied Developmental Psychology: Theory, Practice, and Research from Japan.* Greenwich, Conn.: Information Age Publishing, 2005.

Tomoeda, T., and Suzuki, Y. *Norm Awareness of Contemporary High School Students.* Fukuoka: Kyushu University Publishing, 2003. (in Japanese)

Yamada, T., and others (eds.). *New Meikai Dictionary of Japanese.* Tokyo: Sanseido, 2005. (in Japanese)

Yamagishi, T. *The Structure of Reliance: The Evolution Game of the Mind and Society.* Tokyo: Tokyo University Press, 1998. (in Japanese)

Yamagishi, T. *From a Society of Security to a Society of Trust: The Whereabouts of the Japanese System.* Tokyo: Chuokoron Shinsha, 1999. (in Japanese)

Yamagishi, T., and Yamagishi, M. "Trust and Commitment in the United States and Japan." *Motivation and Emotion,* 1994, *18,* 129–166. (in Japanese)

Yamagishi, T., and others. "Formation of Structure and Commitment—An Experimental Study." *Japanese Journal of Experimental Social Psychology,* 1995, *35,* 23–34. (in Japanese)

SHUJI SUGIE is a professor of teacher education on the Faculty of Liberal Arts, Chukyo University, Nagoya, Japan. An expert on cooperative learning and teacher education, he co-founded and is the director of the Japanese Association for the Study of Cooperation in Education. He has published numerous books and papers on teaching, learning, and educational reform.

DAVID W. SHWALB is on the faculty of the Psychology Department at Southeastern Louisiana University. He is also a research affiliate of the Hokkaido University Faculty of Education and the Japanese Child and Family National Research Center, and has taught and conducted research in Japan for nine years.

BARBARA J. SHWALB teaches in the Psychology Department at Southeastern Louisiana University. She is also a research affiliate of the Hokkaido University Faculty of Education and the Japanese Child and Family National Research Center, and has taught and conducted field research in Japan for six years.

5

Children's peer relations are critical for social adjustment and respect plays an important role in peer relations. Furthermore, children's understanding and expression of respect is related to culture. This chapter discusses the interplay of culture, peer social competence, and respect.

Respect, Liking, and Peer Social Competence in China and the United States

Robert Cohen, Yeh Hsueh, Zongkui Zhou, Miriam H. Hancock, Randy Floyd

Adults often tell children to "show respect" or "be respectful." But how do children understand the concept of respect, and how does it affect their relationships with peers? Can you respect someone you dislike? Can you like someone you do not respect? How does culture influence children's understanding and expression of liking and respect? These questions sparked the research reported in this chapter.

A great deal of empirical research has established the critical function of children's social competence in relationships with peers for their current and subsequent psychosocial and academic adjustment. A cornerstone of this literature concerns the extent to which children like and dislike their peers. Another construct that seems important for children's peer relations, and one that has received little empirical attention to date, is respect. Although the concept of respect historically has been a sidebar in theories of child development, and in spite of frequent references to respect in modern discourse about schools and classroom contexts, this construct has not

The research reported here was supported by a Center of Excellence Grant from the State of Tennessee to the Center for Applied Psychological Research, Department of Psychology, University of Memphis, and by the Excellent Young Teachers Program of the Ministry of Education, People's Republic of China.

NEW DIRECTIONS FOR CHILD AND ADOLESCENT DEVELOPMENT, no. 114, Winter 2006 © Wiley Periodicals, Inc.
Published online in Wiley InterScience (www.interscience.wiley.com) • DOI: 10.1002/cad.175

53

been a focal point of research on children's peer social competence. A primary goal for this chapter is the interplay among the constructs of peer respect, peer liking, and peer social competence.

Children develop in relation to changing participation in the sociocultural activities of their communities, including their community of peers (Rogoff, 2003). A growing body of literature on the features and effects of children's peer social competence is accumulating for children in countries other than the United States. Therefore, a second focal point of this chapter is a cultural examination of peer respect, peer liking, and peer social competence. To build on collaborative research on peer relations begun in 2000 between scholars at the University of Memphis and Central China Normal University, we chose to undertake an assessment of respect among children in the United States and China. We believe that conceptions and evaluations of respect serve as key ingredients in the development of children's peer relations and that the importance of respect as a construct is particularly clear when illuminated in the context of very different cultures.

First, we discuss the importance of children's peer social functioning and a hierarchy of social complexity, as offered by Rubin, Bukowski, and Parker (1998), to organize our thinking about peer relations. Next, we present research on peer social competence across cultures and use cultural schema as an important conceptual tool. Third, we summarize our earlier research on children's understanding of respect, which provided the background for our integration of peer respect, peer liking, and peer social competence. Fourth, we present the results of a project that evaluated peer liking and peer respect for peer social competence of third through sixth graders in the United States and China. We conclude the chapter with a synthesis of our work on the development of peer respect, peer liking, and peer social competence as expressed through the medium of culture.

Importance of Peer Social Functioning

Social competence can be broadly defined as "the ability to achieve personal goals in social interactions while simultaneously maintaining positive relationships with others over time and across situations" (Rubin and Rose-Krasnor, 1992; quoted in Rubin and others, 1998, p. 645). This view of social competence implies a successful balance of agentic goals ("getting ahead") and communal goals ("getting along"; see Wiggins, 1991). From this perspective, aggressive children who may be highly effective in getting what they want but are consequently disliked by the peer group would not be considered socially competent. Similarly, submissive children who get along well with peers but wield no influence over them would also not be viewed as socially competent. In sum, social competence requires a savvy that facilitates individual and social advancement and maintains positive relationships.

NEW DIRECTIONS FOR CHILD AND ADOLESCENT DEVELOPMENT • DOI: 10.1002/cad

A great deal of research has examined individual characteristics in children's social competence with peers, that is, characteristics of children that influence their peer relations, including social skills, self-concept, and social information processing ability (see Crick and Dodge, 1994). As the scope of peer research broadened, Rubin, Bukowski, and Parker (1998) elaborated on Hinde (1992) to provide a useful framework for extending and organizing the complex nature of children's peer social functioning, and thus social competence. Acknowledging the importance of individual characteristics of children, they described three additional hierarchical levels of social complexity important for both current and long-term adjustment: interactions, relationships, and groups. These levels, although influencing each other, are each characterized by unique processes; thus, one cannot fully understand a single level by comprehensively studying levels below it.

Interactions are defined as interdependent dyadic behaviors in which the behavior of one member of a dyad functions as both a stimulus for and a response to the behavior of the other (Rubin, Bukowski, and Parker, 1998). Peer relations researchers have focused primarily on three general categories of social behaviors: moving toward peers (sociability, presumed to also include prosocial behavior), moving against peers (aggression), and moving away from peers (withdrawal). Generally these categories of behavior are highly predictive of acceptance by peers, which in turn are related to several psychosocial outcomes. Specifically, sociable children are more popular with their peers, have more mutual friends, and perform better in school than unsociable children. Social withdrawal, although not associated with negative peer outcomes in early childhood, is linked to rejection by peers and internalizing problems in later childhood. Aggression, which is the most robust predictor of peer rejection, is associated with concurrent and long-term behavioral, emotional, and academic maladjustment.

Relationships imply a history of successive interactions between two people, as well as expectations for future behavior (Rubin, Bukowski, and Parker, 1998). Friendships are perhaps the most studied relationships of children, and mutual friendships, defined as reciprocal nominations for friendship, have received the most attention from researchers. In addition, there is an emerging interest among researchers in enemies or "mutual antipathies," which often are defined as reciprocal classroom nominations for "like least" (Abecassis and others, 2002). Relationships are important for children's social functioning, and researchers have documented the value of friends for promotion of psychosocial adjustment (Bagwell, Newcomb, and Bukowski, 1998; Ladd, 1990) and protection against victimization (Hodges, Boivin, Vitaro, and Bukowski, 1999).

Groups comprise multiple interacting individuals and multiple relationships, across which patterns of social hierarchy emerge (Rubin, Bukowski, and Parker, 1998). The most common assessment of social standing within the peer group are sociometric measures (Coie, Dodge, and Coppotelli,

1982), which reveal status in relation to how much children are liked and disliked by peers. Indexes of social standing include social preference (general likability by peers), social impact (overall visibility in peer group), and categories of sociometric status (popular, rejected, neglected, controversial, or average; Coie, Dodge, and Coppotelli, 1982). Rejection by the peer group is associated with various negative outcomes, including depression, loneliness, conduct problems, poor academic performance, school dropout, substance abuse, delinquency, and adult psychopathology (Rubin, Bukowski, and Parker, 1998).

Culture and Peer Relations

Children's individual characteristics, social interactions, relationships, and group functioning with peers all provide important information about their psychosocial functioning. However, behavior must be considered within a broader sociocultural context, and the meanings and implications of behavior are likely to vary across cultures. Cole (1996) contends that culture is the medium through which behavior acquires meaning. Although the importance of peer social competence appears to be universal, the particular relations between indexes and outcomes often vary across cultures. A brief review of the literature on peer social competence of Chinese children is provided next, with attention to the general similarities and differences in social competence variables between children in American and Chinese cultures.

There are many similarities among American and Chinese descriptions of peer social competence. As is the case with American children, sociable behavior is concurrently and longitudinally related to number of mutual friends and peer acceptance for Chinese children (Chen and others, 2004; Chen, Rubin, and Li, 1995). Also consistent with U.S. research, aggressive children in China generally are rejected by their peers and display more behavioral and academic problems than nonaggressive children, concurrently and over time (Chen and others, 1995, 2004; Xu, Farver, Schwartz, and Chang, 2003). Peer rejection has been associated with depression and externalizing problems for Chinese children (Chen, Rubin, and Li, 1995; Chen and others, 2003).

Despite the many similarities, there are reportedly some differences in the characteristics of social competence in Chinese versus American children. A prominent difference concerns the evaluation of shy/inhibited behaviors across cultures. Although these behaviors are generally associated with peer rejection for American children beginning at about the third grade (Coie, Dodge, and Kupersmidt, 1990), findings for Chinese children are mixed. Some studies suggest that shyness/inhibition is related to positive peer relations and academic adjustment (Chen, Rubin, and Li, 1995; Chen, Rubin, and Sun, 1992); other studies report shyness/inhibition is associated with peer rejection, fewer friendships, victimization, and poor academic adjustment (Schwartz, Chang, and Farver, 2001; Xu, Farver, Schwartz, and Chang, 2003). These contrasting findings for Chinese children may reflect

NEW DIRECTIONS FOR CHILD AND ADOLESCENT DEVELOPMENT • DOI: 10.1002/cad

a historical change in Chinese society. Using longitudinal data, Chen, Cen, Li, and He (2005) reported that shyness/sensitivity was positively related to peer acceptance in a 1990 cohort, positively associated with both peer acceptance and peer rejection in a 1998 cohort, and negatively associated with peer acceptance in a 2002 cohort. Thus, previous discrepant findings about children's peer withdrawal behaviors may reflect generational changes in how peers evaluate these behaviors.

In sum, it appears that the meanings of sociable and aggressive behaviors and the implication of peer rejection are most often the same for American and Chinese children (Chen, Rubin, and Li, 1995). However, these two countries may attach different meanings to the construct of shyness/inhibition, which reflect different historically based cultural values.

How can we best conceptualize our understanding of social functioning through the medium of culture? For many years, the most common interpretation of cultural differences was in terms of the distinction of individualism versus collectivism. Most often, the United States was considered an individualistic society, whereas China was categorized as collectivist in its cultural orientation (Kagitçibasi, 1997). Although this framework facilitates a categorical understanding of cultural behaviors, it does not apply well when we seek to understand within-culture variation. Neither does this dichotomy provide the basis for analysis of developmental issues or cultural change over time. Therefore, we prefer the theoretical construct of cultural schema, as propagated by cognitive anthropologists, as our interpretive tool.

A cultural schema is "a conceptual structure which makes possible the identification of objects and events" (D'Andrade, 1992, p. 28) through omnipresent cultural mediation (Cole, 1996). Based on this framework, we posit that a cultural schema for knowing and showing respect develops as a result of culture-specific child-rearing practices. It is composed of a system of cultural symbols and artifacts organized in a hierarchical cognitive structure that develops in childhood. For example, at the age of four or five, Chinese children already believe that effort is more important than ability for learning (Li, 2003a). Also in the preschool years, American children's self-concept is centered on personal feelings and positive traits, in marked contrast to Chinese children's self-concept, which is centered on their social roles (Wang, 2004). Cultural schemas are not considered to be personal conceptual structures but are shared among people in the culture (Markus, Kitayama, and Heiman, 1998). The symbolic contents of cultural schemas provide the framework for children to interpret relationships in a classroom or to understand appropriate ways to respect a teacher. Cultural schemas provide a conceptual tool to focus on culturally mediated meaning for understanding variations within or between cultures.

Much of the literature on cultural similarities and differences in peer relations is biased due to the nature of the instruments and the lack of cultural grounding of theories. Specifically, most cultural research on peer relations makes cross-cultural comparisons using instruments developed in the

West rather than being guided by cultural concepts and field-based analysis. However, these studies make a contribution by promoting an increasingly culturally appropriate approach to understand children's peer relations in different cultural contexts. Our own research relating peer relations to children's understanding of the concept of respect in the United States and China applies a cultural perspective.

Children's Understanding of Respect

As Frei and Shaver (2002) noted, "Little effort has been made to define respect, measure it, or discover how it relates to other relationship constructs" (p. 121). Piaget (1962) suggested that children first learn about respect in relationships with parents, where respect is an expression of a unilateral respect. According to Piaget's view, as children enter middle childhood, peers become an important influence on their learning about and sustaining mutual respect (Lightfoot, 2000; Piaget, 1962).

Two cross-cultural studies have directly investigated respect for teachers. The first found that twelve-year-old Japanese and Australian children believed, to a comparable degree, that they should respect teachers (Mann, Mitsui, Beswick, and Harmoni, 1994). The other study (Taylor, Wilson, Kaneda, and Ogawa, 2000) asked Japanese and American first and second graders what they would do if wrongfully accused of cheating. Two-thirds of the Japanese children responded that they would insist on their honesty without verbalizing a reason, while nine of ten American children reported they would give a reason to show they were wronged. Together these two studies investigated unilateral respect toward teachers by children and revealed cultural differences in how children evaluated this type of respect. As Li (2003b) has suggested, respect is a conscious construct of human relationships that is contextualized by a set of cultural values and beliefs.

The purpose of our research was to evaluate the role of peer respect in children's peer relations. Before making this connection, we believed that it was necessary to examine children's understanding of the construct of respect. We wanted a culturally relevant instrument, based on information from children themselves, that would be relevant to the study of mutual respect and peer relations. We began by interviewing children in China and the United States. The interview consisted of a number of open-ended questions about the definition, function, and behavioral expression of respect. A research team consisting of three university faculty members, two of whom were from China, and six American psychology graduate students evaluated the transcripts of all responses. Forming a consensus, the research team worded alternatives that they felt best reflected the contents of children's responses.

We developed a three-item questionnaire with each item having five alternative responses (Hsueh and others, 2005). This questionnaire was translated into Chinese and, as a check, was back-translated into English.

The first question was about the definition of the word *respect:* "What does the word *respect* mean?" The second question evaluated the reasons for which one respects others: "Why should we respect others?" And the third question concerned the child's view of how one showed respect to one's teacher: "Your mother tells you one morning on the way to school, 'I want you to be sure to show respect to your teacher when you are at school.' What does *respect your teacher* mean?" The modal responses of children from each cultural sample were as follows.

Three-quarters of American children defined *respect* in terms of reciprocity: "To be good to others and treat them as you want to be treated." Similarly, over one-third gave as a reason for showing respect that "if you respect them, they will respect you," and another third gave a reason having to do with deservingness: "People deserve respect no matter who they are." A sizable percentage of American children, 38 percent, reported that the way to show respect to a teacher was to obey.

Nearly half of Chinese children defined *respect* in terms of admiration ("To look up to or admire someone"), and another 30 percent defined it as reciprocity. Over 40 percent of Chinese children chose deservingness as the reason for showing respect: "People deserve respect no matter who they are." Finally, one-third of Chinese children responded that working hard on school work was the way to show respect to a teacher.

Chinese and American children showed some similarities by defining respect in relation to reciprocity and by giving deservingness as a reason for showing respect. However, the differences between American and Chinese children were striking. First, differences emerged in a greater emphasis on reciprocity by American children and the greater emphasis on admiration by Chinese children. Second, differences were especially evident in beliefs about showing respect for teachers; obedience was important for many American children, and doing one's duty (work hard) was more commonly expressed by Chinese children.

Hsueh and others (2005) documented children's understanding of the definition of respect, the function of respect, and the behavioral expression of showing respect. As discussed at length in that article, we believe that children's understanding is best understood in relation to the medium of culture, specifically in reference to cultural schema. We also believe that it is timely and appropriate to evaluate peer respect as an important contributor to peer social functioning.

Evaluating Peer Respect, Peer Liking, and Social Competence

We have considered the importance of children's peer relations to concurrent and subsequent adjustment, culture as a medium for understanding peer relations, and our research on children's understanding of respect. This discussion set the stage for the presentation of our latest research, which examined American and Chinese children's peer social competence, peer liking, and peer respect.

The thesis of this research was that showing respect and being respected by others are important for the regulation of interpersonal relationships. We believed that the relations among social competence, peer liking, and peer respect would be reflected differently by children in the United States versus China, particularly given the differences in the understanding of respect from our previous work. In addition, we believed that respect would serve as an important determinant for peer evaluations for children in both cultures; thus, we hypothesized that peer respect would mediate the relation between social competence and peer liking.

As part of a larger longitudinal study, we assessed self and peer reports of social competence for 580 (318 boys, 262 girls) children in Wuhan, China, and 235 (109 boys, 126 girls) children in Memphis, Tennessee. Children were enrolled in grades 3 through 6 at a university-affiliated public school in each country and were considered as living in middle-class families in their respective countries. In the Memphis sample, approximately half the participants were African Americans and half were European Americans. All measures were originally developed in the United States; many have been used extensively in China. Each measure was translated into Chinese and tested for accuracy by translating back into English.

Correlations Among Measures. Peer nominations for respect and for liking (children were asked to circle the names of all the children in the class they liked/respected on separate classroom roster) were significantly and positively correlated for both cultures, Chinese r (580) = .69, $p < .001$; U.S. r (235) = .49, $p < .001$. The association was significantly higher for the Chinese children than the American children ($z = 4.01$, $p < .001$). Thus, as expected, peer respect was closely associated with peer liking. In addition, these constructs were considerably more fused and overlapping for the Chinese participants than the American participants.

Peer liking and peer respect were correlated with the other peer social competence variables for each group of children; the results are summarized in Table 5.1. The patterns of significant correlations were similar for peer liking nominations for children in China and children in the United States. Specifically, for both groups, there were significant correlations with peer liking for the same five (out of eight) measures: self-perceived social competence, loneliness (negative correlation), peer optimism, number of mutual friends, and sociability behavior nominations. There were two differences between groups of children. Peer liking was positively correlated with friendship quality for children in China but was not significantly correlated for children in the United States. Second, peer liking was negatively correlated with withdrawn peer behavior nominations for children in the United States, but, consistent with Chen, Rubin, and Li (1995) and Chen, Rubin, and Sun (1992), was not significantly correlated for children in China.

Table 5.1. Correlations between Peer Respect Nominations and Peer Liking Nominations with Other Social Competence Measures

	China		United States	
Social Competence Measure	Peer Respect	Peer Liking	Peer Respect	Peer Liking
Self-perceived social competence	.17	.22	—	.30
Loneliness	−.28	−.31	—	−.23
Peer optimism	.26	.27	—	.25
Friendship quality	.21	.23	—	—
Number of mutual classroom friends	.54	.62	.42	.46
Peer nominations for sociability behaviors	.91	.68	.69	.59
Peer nominations for aggression behavior	—	—	−.45	—
Peer nominations for withdrawn behaviors	—	—	—	−.29

Note: Cells with numbers represent significant correlations, $p < .05$.

The patterns of significant correlations between peer respect and the other social competence measures were fairly distinct between the two cultures. For children in China, the pattern was exactly the same as that shown between peer liking and the social competence variables. This similarity is perhaps another indication of a greater fusion of the constructs of liking and respect for children in China but not the United States, as proposed above. For children in the United States, only three correlations between peer respect and the other peer social competence variables were statistically significant. Nominations of respect from peers were positively correlated with number of mutual friends and with sociability behavior nominations and negatively correlated with aggression behavior nominations. For children in the United States, peer respect nominations were not significantly correlated with any of the self-report measures of social competence as they had been with the peer liking nominations.

Modeling Peer Social Competence, Peer Respect, and Peer Liking. We constructed a series of conceptual models for children in China and children in the United States using Amos 5.0 (Arbuckle and Wothke, 2004). We analyzed the specified latent-variable models through the process of confirmatory factor analysis and structural equation modeling. First, using confirmatory factor analysis, we constructed a measurement model, dividing the social competence measures into two latent variables: self-report measures and peer report or relationship-related measures. Two adjustments to our original model were required: aggression and withdrawn behavior nominations by peers were dropped from the models. For children from both cultures, by all indexes of goodness of fit between the conceptual models and the actual relations in the data, the measures of social competence significantly mapped onto these self and peer constructs of social competence represented by latent variables.

We then assessed two models: (1) peer liking as a mediator between the social competence latent variables (self and peer) and peer respect and (2) peer respect as a mediator between the social competence latent variables (self and peer) and peer liking. For children in both cultures, the model using peer respect as a mediator between social competence and peer liking was the better-fitting model. In fact, the model of respect mediating liking showed acceptable measures of fit for all indexes for both groups of children, and the model of liking mediating respect did not show acceptable fit.

Summary. Three sets of findings relating peer social competence, peer liking, and peer respect were the same between children in China and children in the United States. Regardless of culture, nominations for peer liking and nominations for peer respect were positively associated. Second, the relations of peer nominations for liking with the other social competence variables were quite similar. Finally, again regardless of culture, the relation of social competence to peer liking was mediated by peer respect.

Cultural variations appeared as well. Children in China, relative to children in the United States, showed a significantly greater positive correlation of peer liking with peer respect. In addition, patterns of correlations between social competence variables with peer liking and with peer respect were more similar for children in China than children in the United States. In fact, children in China showed the same pattern of correlations for both sets of correlations. For American children, the patterns were quite different. In particular, peer respect did not significantly correlate with the self-report social competence measures.

Thus far, we have interpreted the findings of this research in terms of cultural similarities and differences. In the next, and final section, we return to our goal of establishing the relations among peer respect, peer liking, and peer social competence, as expressed through the medium of culture.

Respect, Liking, Peer Social Competence, and Culture

Peer social competence has been shown to be an extremely important predictor of both current and subsequent adjustment in children's development. Specifically, how children are evaluated by peers in terms of peer liking is a key index of social functioning. The research presented here advocates for the inclusion of peer respect as an important variable mediating peer liking. In addition, peer respect (and peer liking) should be examined through the medium of culture.

Our findings suggest that respect serves the role of mediator between a fairly large set of self and peer reports of social competence and peer liking. That is, peer liking relates to social competence variables as reflected through considerations of peer respect. The strong correlation between liking and respect suggests that although children may respect someone they dislike, or they may like someone they do not respect, they generally like those whom they respect.

NEW DIRECTIONS FOR CHILD AND ADOLESCENT DEVELOPMENT • DOI: 10.1002/cad

Recall from our previous work (Hsueh and others, 2005) that American and Chinese children have different understandings of the definition, function, and behavioral expression of respect. Generally children in the United States viewed respect in terms of reciprocity, that is, a belief that there is a give and take to respect within interpersonal relations. Children in China view respect as inherent in the social order, i.e., respect is not earned but rather, it is part of the fabric of interpersonal relations. Given these cultural differences, it is not surprising that children in China revealed a closer association between considerations of peer liking and peer respect. Furthermore, relative to the American children, children in China who were more respected also were more likely to report more positive self-functioning and receive more positive peer behavior nominations than children who were less respected. In short, respect was important for positive social functioning for both American and Chinese children. However, for the children in China, peer respect was a more core concept for the organization of social activities than it was for children in the United States.

A word of caution is needed. We have used the term *culture* throughout this chapter. China and the United States are countries with a great deal of diversity. We studied children in Memphis, Tennessee, and Wuhan, China. There are many equivalences between these groups: both are from medium-sized cities, on a major river, in the center of their respective countries, associated with college campuses, and generally middle-class socioeconomic status. However, no one should make the assumption that we chose representative samples of American and Chinese children.

We suggest that Hinde's (1992) and Rubin, Bukowski, and Parker's (1998) levels of social complexity provide a useful structure for understanding children's peer relations regardless of culture. Children's individual social dispositions and characteristics, their social interactions, their social relationships, and their peer group participation dynamically and jointly determine social outcomes. These are the forms for engaging in peer social activities. Culture permeates the content within this structure. Particular individual characteristics, interactions, relationships, and peer group participation will have different meaning and different outcomes dependent on the culture within which these social phenomena are expressed and understood. Regardless of culture, peer liking is related to a wide variety of peer social competence measures, as mediated by peer respect. But the particular relations between peer respect and other variables are dependent on the medium of culture.

In conclusion, peer relations are critically important for self and social functioning, and being liked by peers is a powerful index of peer relations. We contend that being respected by peers is another key component of peer relations, not simply as a correlate of peer liking but also as a factor that mediates the association of a variety of peer social competence variables and peer liking. Finally, although social complexity at the levels of individual, interactions, relationships, and groups provides a useful and universal structure within which to examine children's peer relations, one

NEW DIRECTIONS FOR CHILD AND ADOLESCENT DEVELOPMENT • DOI: 10.1002/cad

must address the relations among particular peer social competence variables through the medium of culture.

References

Abecassis, M., and others. "Mutual Antipathies and Their Significance in Middle Childhood and Adolescence." *Child Development,* 2002, *73,* 1543–1556.

Arbuckle, J. L., and Wothke, W. *Amos 5.0 User's Guide.* Chicago: Smallwaters, 2004.

Bagwell, C. L., Newcomb, A. F., and Bukowski, W. M. "Preadolescent Friendship and Peer Rejection as Predictors of Adult Adjustment." *Child Development,* 1998, *69,* 140–153.

Chen, X., Cen, G., Li, D., and He, Y. "Social Functioning and Adjustment in Chinese Children: The Imprint of Historical Time." *Child Development,* 2005, *76,* 182–195.

Chen, X., Rubin, K. H., and Sun, Y. "Social Reputation and Peer Relationships in Chinese and Canadian Children: A Cross-Cultural Study." *Child Development,* 1992, *63,* 1336–1343.

Chen, X., Rubin, K., and Li, Z. "Social Functioning and Adjustment in Chinese Children: A Longitudinal Study." *Developmental Psychology,* 1995, *31,* 531–539.

Chen, X., and others. "Parental Reports of Externalizing and Internalizing Behaviors in Chinese Children: Relevancy to Social, Emotional and School Adjustment." *Journal of Psychology in Chinese Societies,* 2003, *3,* 233–259.

Chen, X., and others. "Loneliness and Social Adaptation in Brazilian, Canadian, Chinese and Italian Children: A Multi-National Comparative Study." *Journal of Child Psychology and Psychiatry,* 2004, *45(8),* 1373–1384.

Coie, J. D., Dodge, K. A., and Coppotelli, H. "Dimensions and Types of Social Status: A Cross-Age Perspective." *Developmental Psychology,* 1982, *18,* 557–570.

Coie, J. D., Dodge, K. A., and Kupersmidt, J. B. "Peer Group Behavior and Social Status." In S. R. Asher and J. D. Coie (eds.), *Peer Rejection in Childhood.* Cambridge, U.K.: Cambridge University Press, 1990.

Cole, M. *Cultural Psychology: A Once and Future Discipline.* Cambridge, Mass.: Harvard University Press, 1996.

Crick, N. R., and Dodge, K. A. "A Review and Reformulation of Social Information-Processing Mechanisms in Children's Social Adjustment." *Psychological Bulletin,* 1994, *115,* 74–101.

D'Andrade, R. G. "Schemas and Motivation." In R. G. D'Andrade and C. Strauss (eds.), *Human Motives and Cultural Models.* Cambridge: Cambridge University Press, 1992.

Frei, J. R., and Shaver, P. R. "Respect in Close Relationships: Prototype Definition, Self-Report Assessment, and Initial Correlates." *Personal Relationships,* 2002, *9,* 121–139.

Hinde, R. A. "Developmental Psychology in the Context of Other Behavioral Sciences." *Developmental Psychology,* 1992, *28,* 1018–1029.

Hodges, E., Boivin, M., Vitaro, F., and Bukowski, W. "The Power of Friendship: Protection Against an Escalating Cycle of Peer Victimization." *Developmental Psychology,* 1999, *35,* 94–101.

Hsueh, Y., and others. "Knowing and Showing Respect: Chinese and U.S. Children's Understanding of Respect and Its Association to Their Friendships." *Journal of Psychology in Chinese Societies,* 2005, *6,* 229-260.

Kagitçibasi, C. "Individualism and Collectivism." In J. W. Berry, M. H. Segall, and C. Kagitçibasi (eds.), *Handbook of Cross-Cultural Psychology.* (2nd ed.) Needham Heights, Mass.: Allyn and Bacon, 1997.

Ladd, G. W. "Having Friends, Keeping Friends, Making Friends, and Being Liked by Peers in the Classroom: Predictors of Children's Early School Adjustment?" *Child Development,* 1990, *61,* 312–331.

Li, J. "U.S. and Chinese Cultural Beliefs About Learning." *Journal of Educational Psychology*, 2003a, *95*, 258–267.

Li, J. "The Core of Confucian Learning." *American Psychologist*, 2003b, *58*, 146–147.

Lightfoot, C. "On Respect." *New Ideas in Psychology*, 2000, *18*, 177–185.

Mann, L., Mitsui, H., Beswick, G., and Harmoni, R. "A Study of Japanese and Australian Children's Respect for Others." *Journal of Cross-Cultural Psychology*, 1994, *25*, 133–145.

Markus, H. R., Kitayama, S., and Heiman, R. J. "Collective Self-Schemas: The Sociocultural Ground of the Personal." In U. Neisser and D. Jopling (eds.), *The Conceptual Self in Context: Culture, Experience, Self-Understanding*. Cambridge, U.K.: Cambridge University Press, 1998.

Piaget, J. *The Moral Judgment of the Child*. New York: Collier, 1962. (Originally published in 1932.)

Rogoff, B. *The Cultural Nature of Human Development*. New York: Oxford University Press, 2003.

Rubin, K. H., Bukowski, W., and Parker, J. G. "Peer Interactions, Relationships, and Groups." In W. Damon (ed. in chief) and N. Eisenberg (volume ed.), *Handbook of Child Psychology*. Vol. 3: *Social, Emotional and Personality Development*. (5th ed.) New York: Wiley, 1998.

Rubin, K., and Rose-Krasnor, L. "Interpersonal Problem Solving." In V. B. Van Hassett and M. Herses (eds.), *Handbook of Social Development*. New York: Plenum Press, 1992.

Schwartz, D., Chang, L., and Farver, J. M. "Correlates of Victimization in Chinese Children's Peer Groups." *Developmental Psychology*, 2001, *37*, 520–532.

Taylor, S. I., Wilson, J. T., Kaneda, T., and Ogawa, T. "Rules Are Made to Be Golden: A Qualitative Study of American and Japanese Children's Morals." *Kindergarten Education: Theory, Research, and Practice*, 2000, *5*, 19–41.

Wang, Q. "The Emergence of Cultural Self-Constructs: Autobiographical Memory and Self-Description in European American and Chinese Children." *Developmental Psychology*, 2004, *40*, 3–15.

Wiggins, J. S. "Agency and Communion as Conceptual Coordinates for the Understanding and Measurement of Interpersonal Behavior." In W. Grove and D. Cicchetti (eds.), *Thinking Clearly About Psychology: Essays in Honor of Paul Meehl*. Minneapolis: University of Minnesota Press, 1991.

Xu, Y., Farver, J. M., Schwartz, D., and Chang, L. "Identifying Aggressive Victims in Chinese Children's Peer Groups." *International Journal of Behavioral Development*, 2003, *27*, 243–252.

ROBERT COHEN *is a professor in the Department of Psychology, University of Memphis, Tennessee.*

YEH HSUEH *is a professor in the Department of Counseling, Educational Psychology, and Research, University of Memphis, Tennessee.*

ZONGKUI ZHOU *is a professor in the Department of Psychology, Central China Normal University, Wuhan, China.*

MIRIAM H. HANCOCK *is a doctoral student in the Department of Psychology, University of Memphis, Tennessee.*

RANDY FLOYD *is an assistant professor in the Department of Psychology, University of Memphis, Tennessee.*

*The developmental origins of respect and disrespect
among American children are seen in early childhood
and in the transition to the school years. This chapter
presents the first published research to focus on the
development of both respect and disrespect as distinct
concepts. The findings are examined in the context of
both sociocultural and Piagetian theories.*

Concept Development of Respect and Disrespect in American Kindergarten and First- and Second-Grade Children

Barbara J. Shwalb, David W. Shwalb

"In the beginning was the Word," begins the New Testament Gospel of St. John. The theory of Lev Vygotsky supports this statement as applicable to the process of how formation of the concepts of respect and disrespect begin with "the word." When they are very young, children are exposed to words whose definitions come from a wide language domain. They must then determine the concept of a word's meaning in a dynamic process that is influenced by each child's cognitive and social development. We view respect and disrespect as spontaneous concepts that change according to the norms of cultures and subcultures (Vygotsky, 1962).

In this chapter, we explore the development of the concepts of respect and disrespect in early and middle childhood. Because there had been only one published empirical study about the early childhood origins of respect (Piaget, 1932) and none about disrespect, we begin with a general discussion of how the development of these concepts may be rooted in the preschool years. Then we report preliminary results from our research on

We extend our appreciation to the children and teachers of the Southeastern Louisiana University Laboratory School (Beth Robinson, director) for their participation, and to Highlights for Children, Inc., for permission to use the stimulus materials. This chapter is dedicated with respect to our parents.

children's thinking about respect and disrespect and how it changes in the transition to middle childhood. Throughout the chapter, we pay attention to three aspects of respect and disrespect (cognitive, affective, and behavioral) and on how children's thinking may change with age in relation to cultural, environmental, and historical factors. We studied these concepts among the residents of a small town in the United States and have drawn on ideas from Piaget's *The Moral Judgment of the Child* (1932) and Vygotsky's *Thought and Language* (1962).

Definitions of spontaneous concepts consist of meanings that are useful for most adults, even though the particular words that describe a concept have murky connections to other words. Compared with spontaneous concepts like respect and disrespect, Vygotsky (1962) wrote that natural concepts, such as gravity, are more quickly understood by children, since children generally encounter natural concepts with accompanying definitions. Because spontaneous concepts are dynamic, we expect their meanings to change over time and in the context of different populations and communities, but not so quickly as to replace the concepts' past meanings.

We believe that the core meanings of respect and disrespect in the American context are widely understood by almost all Americans. At the same time, the concepts of respect and disrespect are embedded within different schemas in different American subcultures. For example, some Latino Americans show respect to their ancestors on All Souls Day in a joyous and reverent gathering at a grave site. Another example of showing respect is the widespread use among southern Americans of the words *sir* and *ma'am* when addressing others. But although these behaviors are unique to particular groups, the people who populate both groups understand respect and disrespect in ways much more similar than dissimilar because they are all Americans.

Most Americans are also aware of certain clusters of words they use to refine and define what is encapsulated in the words and the concepts of respect and disrespect and what is not. We assert that despite variations, there is an overall consensus within American society about the general meaning of the words *respect* and *disrespect,* and there is a normative developmental conceptual pathway that leads to the collective understanding of these words. If a population of people did not attach similar meanings to the words *respect* and *disrespect,* then these two words would no longer be used in everyday communications.

For the past three years, we have begun to immerse ourselves in an exploration of the normative developmental pathways associated with the words *respect* and *disrespect* (Shwalb and others, 2006). We have found limited relevant source materials in the literatures of psychology and other sciences, communicated with professionals with similar interests, and conducted research on age groups from childhood through adulthood. This chapter introduces some of what we learned about the normative developmental course of the concepts of respect and disrespect from American children in kindergarten and first and second grades.

The Developmental Trajectory of Respect and Disrespect

In this section, we outline the general pathways during early and middle childhood by which the words *respect* and *disrespect* become concepts within the multiple contextual systems of American culture. We examine three aspects of respect and disrespect (cognitive, behavioral, affective) and two developmental stages (early childhood and middle childhood).

Three Aspects of Development. Cognitive, behavioral, and affective aspects of respect and disrespect merge as these concepts emerge in early childhood.

Cognitive. From a sociocultural perspective, learning the meaning of a word is a spectator sport for a young child. The child cannot meaningfully interact with a word without sufficient information processing capabilities to perceive that the word has a referent situation. As the child's neurological and cognitive capabilities mature, the concept of a word's meaning will make continual conceptual shifts as mediated by the child's cognitions and environment (Vygotsky, 1962). Ideas do not create themselves, and therefore ideas related to respect and disrespect are originally dependent on what the child's parents, other caregivers, their surroundings, and the mass media provide as examples. Respect and disrespect are not the types of concepts a child acquires from other people as one-word summaries; they are typically illustrated by example. For instance, a child may encounter examples of respect such as not to interrupt the conversations of adults, to take care of one's toys, and to use a quiet voice in public places. The diverse situations in which the concept has meaning might make it difficult for this child to quickly categorize meanings, and the concept will acquire a quality of generalizability.

Behavioral. Generalizability in the acquisition of the concepts of respect and disrespect leads a child to recognize and perform specific behaviors that represent the concepts. This process is similar to "spread of effect" (Thorndike, 1932) in that generalizability focuses the child's attention on finding examples of the concept in daily life. The child actively directs his or her thinking to find similar examples. Children also learn readily from the use of opposites, and so their cognitive attention is engaged to perceive behaviors that do not represent a concept. As the child develops a cache of examples representing respect and a different cache representing disrespect, he or she builds a catalogue of hierarchical saliency for the examples under the direction of socialization agents such as parents. We presume that the child has no innate ability to know to what degree a behavioral example is salient to a concept. Therefore, a source outside the child must convey, for example, that it is more representative of respect to give up a bus seat to an elderly rider than to give the bus seat to a teenage rider. Acquisition of the concepts of respect and disrespect enables a child to seek out and learn respectful and disrespectful behaviors.

Affective. We further posit that the words *respect* and *disrespect* in their earliest presentations are related to children's behavioral regulation, and as a result these words quickly acquire affective significance. That is, the parental affective tendencies, such as using a sharp voice when the child is told not to interrupt adult conversations or smiling at the child who holds a door open, are conveyed to the child as meaningful elements of the concepts themselves. The affective qualities of the concepts *respect* and *disrespect* assume increasing importance to children across the school years, and into adolescence and adulthood, as they learn that respect is often (if not always) associated with pleasant, harmonious relationships, and disrespect is often related to unpleasant, discordant relationships. In sum, the concepts of respect and disrespect in American society develop within a structural network that links cognition, behavior, and emotion.

Transition to Middle Childhood. We assert that the development linkage of behavioral, cognitive, and affective aspects of respect and disrespect occurs from the preschool years through adolescence.

Early Childhood. No systematic research has focused on the development of American children's conceptual understanding of respect or disrespect in the contexts of homes or preschools. Piaget (1932) discussed the origins of respect among Western European preschool-age children as a corollary to his focus on moral reasoning. He did not directly explore children's conceptualizations of respect, but did provide an elaboration of his own concept of respect. Respect in early childhood, which Piaget termed "unilateral," reflected a compliant attitude and behavior of children toward the authority of their parents. Piaget's concept of respect was compatible with the prevalent thinking of American adults and psychologists of that era. For example, Dollard and others (1939) wrote about the frustrations American children experienced during their socialization process. They noted that as children increasingly took verbal control of their environment and increased in self-control, they came to conceptualize that they should have the same freedoms as adults. Dollard and his colleagues instructed parents that it was adults' responsibility to teach children that they cannot do all the things that adults do and that children must accept their subordinate status and corresponding roles in an agreeable (respectful) manner.

We believe that was the normative view of raising children in American homes sixty-five years ago. In the year 2006, however, children's behavioral upbringing is more multicontextual and diversified than it was in the 1930s. For example, few children in Dollard's generation experienced two to four years of preschool, and even radio was a new source of information then. In the town where we did the research described in this chapter, 1940s telephone directories and newspapers listed no preschool facilities. Television broadcasting on hundreds of channels on a 24/7 basis was unimaginable then, even in science fiction. In the not so distant past, we believe that Americans learned the concepts of respect and disrespect as rooted in the family and neighborhood, and generalizability of these concepts was limited until the child had more social contacts in elementary school.

In the twenty-first century, American children's information about respect behaviors and disrespect behaviors comes from a wide variety of sources. Preschools and day care settings now expose children to a more diverse range of socialization agents and behaviors than previous generations experienced. This is significant because children between the ages of two and six identify strongly with the behavior-and-consequence sequences of their peers. In the past, when children's lives centered around the home until they entered school, there was rarely another person in the household of the same age. Relationships with older or younger siblings do not have the same impact on personal conceptual meaning for the child as when the child spends many hours daily with peers. Television, music, video games, and books are also sources of information that bear on the development of prekindergarten children's concepts of respect and disrespect. American preschoolers watch a great deal of television, and information garnered from this source may strongly influence their knowledge of the concepts of respect and disrespect.

Transition to Middle Childhood. Piaget's observations (1932) led him to postulate a transition in middle childhood to mutual respect, in the context of democratic and egalitarian same-age peer groups. But there has been, until recently (see Chapter Five, this volume) no empirical verification of Piaget's notion of unilateral versus mutual respect. We believe that the concepts of respect and disrespect are far more complex, multidimensional, and multicontextual than the two types Piaget described. We assert that American children enter kindergarten with psychological structures of meaning for respect and for disrespect. One form of information processing that we presume has developed by this point is a deliberative type of thinking that is under the conscious awareness and control of the child. We could therefore ask children, "Does this show respect?" or "Does this show disrespect?" and infer from their answers the nature of their thinking.

By kindergarten, children's vocabulary and verbal fluency have typically reached a level at which, according to our pretesting, they can verbalize their conceptualizations of respect and disrespect. The structure of meaning for respect and disrespect also involves an affective component. Cognition and emotion function together as children interpret their personal and collective environments (Lewis and Haviland-Jones, 2000). Accordingly, we looked at behavior, behavioral intent, words, and affective evaluations of behavior as units of analysis to measure children's understanding and feelings about respect and disrespect.

A Study of Children's Understanding

To investigate how the concepts of respect and disrespect emerge in early childhood and middle childhood, we conducted a quasi-experiment with all the students, ages six through fourteen, at a school in southeastern Louisiana.

Participants. We interviewed 450 children at one elementary school (50 children per grade level, kindergarten through eighth grade), in a suburban town with a population of 30,000. The school was under the administration of the local public school system but housed as a laboratory school on the campus of a state university. There were equal numbers of boys and girls at the school, and the student population was roughly 75 percent European American and 25 percent African American. Of the three grade levels reported on in this chapter, the kindergarten was in a self-contained classroom, while the first and second grades met in an open classroom environment. We anticipated that the responses of first- and second-grade children about respect and disrespect would be both similar, due to their shared experiences within American culture, and also dissimilar due to individual differences in the children's cognitive and affective information processing.

Materials. The concepts of respect and disrespect were depicted in illustrations adapted from issues of the popular magazine, *Highlights for Children.* Five "Goofus and Gallant" feature strips were the stimuli for our experiment. The Goofus and Gallant vignettes teach children about the norms of American society by giving examples of two boys who act in opposite ways. If, for example, Goofus's picture showed excluding a child from a play group, Gallant's picture would show welcoming the same child into the play group. A one-sentence caption accompanied each picture. For instance, the captions for the preceding example read, "Goofus doesn't want the child to play with the group" and "Gallant wants the child to play with the group."

In each of our individual research interviews, a child would respond either to only the five respect pictures (Gallant's) or only to the five disrespect pictures (Goofus's). Each set of five pictures represented situations that the child would be familiar with as normal experiences of childhood. The feature strip themes and pictures were (1) asking/not asking to use other people's possessions, (2) taking care/not taking care of pets, (3) sharing/not sharing the school group's supplies, (4) watching out/not watching out for the welfare of others, and (5) obeying/not obeying classroom rules of conduct. Each child also rated each picture to indicate how respectful or how disrespectful he or she thought each behavior was.

Procedures. Our interviews took the form of, "If yes, then why?" questioning. After we showed each child a clearly drawn and unambiguous picture and read the caption, we asked, "Is this an example of respect behavior?" if the child being interviewed was seeing only the respect (Gallant) pictures. To the children who were shown only the disrespect (Goofus) pictures we asked, "Is this an example of disrespect behavior?" If the child thought the picture was representative of the concept and answered yes to

NEW DIRECTIONS FOR CHILD AND ADOLESCENT DEVELOPMENT • DOI: 10.1002/cad

either question, we then asked the child, "Why?" The words *respect* and *disrespect*, as mentioned earlier, have the quality of generalizabilty. Accordingly, if the child generalized that the words *respect* and *disrespect* were linked in meaning to other concepts, such as good or bad, the child's positive or negative identification of the behavior in the picture would show knowledge by generalization of the target concepts.

Kindergarten Results. The responses of kindergarten children indicated that respect as a concept is rooted in early childhood.

Respect. Overall, the main characteristic of the kindergarten (six-year olds) data was that they demonstrated these children's recognition of the concepts of respect and disrespect in a variety of situations depicted by pictures and captions. Six of twenty-five children did not know that to ask permission to use other people's property was a respect behavior. They responded no when asked if the statement and corresponding picture, "Grandma, may I try out your binoculars?" was a respect behavior. Six kindergarten children also did not recognize that following a classroom rule to raise your hand before speaking was a respect behavior. Another characteristic of kindergartners' answers was their tendency to explain why a situation was an example of a respect behavior without connecting the explanation concretely (relationally) to the picture that they were looking at. The majority of responses to the question, "Why do you think this is an example of respect behavior?" related to the value of their friends, for instance, "So friends remain friends," "Because they are friends," or "So he doesn't lose friends." Kindergartners' concept of respect was most related to friend relationships. Respectfulness has been shown to be vitally important in peer relationships in childhood (see Chapter Five, this volume), adolescents (Yelsma and Yelsma, 1998), and young adults (Nguyen, 2006), but our data were the first to demonstrate its significance as early as in kindergarten. Parents and teachers understand that their role as authority is challenged in direct proportion to a child's needs for peer acceptance, when behavioral goals differ between adults and children. Our data suggest that within a span of two generations in America, this youthful challenge to adult authority has shifted from adolescents in junior high school to six year olds in kindergarten.

A third common feature of kindergartners' concept of respect was that they paid more attention to the perceived personal characteristics of the person in the pictures than they did to the situations. Kindergartners repeatedly said the pictures showed respect because, "He is nice" and "He is good." We believe that the children were equating the word *nice* to merit or worth and that, "He is good," referred to compliance. Their view of compliance was that it was pleasurable, which is counter to the notion that children find compliance to be a disagreeable experience. A fourth trend among kindergarten students was to give affirmative examples rather than negative examples to explain why a situation should be considered respect behavior. Almost 85 percent of their responses to respect situations were explained by saying, "This is respect because . . ." rather than, "This is respect because *he doesn't . . .*" We believe that this is an indication that six year olds have had more familiarity with respect behaviors than with disrespect behaviors. If the children had given similar percentages of affirmative and negative examples to explain a situation, we could assume that their development of the concepts of respect and disrespect was comparable and that the children had approximately the same exposure to positive and negative examples of the behaviors that they were questioned about.

A fifth tendency was not to explain respect as based on fear of punishment. If children had viewed respectful compliance as reflecting preconventional moral reasoning (Kohlberg, 1963), they would have explained respect behaviors as a way of avoiding punishment. But this was not the case. Out of 125 total reasons given by 25 kindergarten children for their cognitions of respect behavior (five different respect pictures shown to each child), only 8 reasons described fear of punishment as the impetus for respect behavior.

Disrespect. Findings on children's understanding of disrespect revealed different tendencies than did the data for respect behavior. For example, six out of twenty-five kindergartners did not think that mistreating a pet was an example of disrespect behavior. Two did not think that shouting in class, taking parents' things without asking permission, or letting a door slam shut on the person behind them were examples of disrespect behaviors. Explanations of disrespect behaviors were more concrete and more situation specific than were explanations for respect behaviors. There were also more rule-specific explanations for disrespect behaviors than for respect behaviors. Examples were, "He's supposed to [share, be nice, ask, or follow rules]." There were few commonalities among the kindergarten children's explanations of why particular behaviors showed disrespect. This adds further support to our belief that the American kindergartners in our study had generally not been exposed to disrespect behaviors in their shared common experiences before kindergarten. Alternatively, if they had seen or heard about disrespect behaviors, the behaviors were dismissed or were irrelevant to them. That is, learning about disrespect lagged behind what children had learned about respect. Overall, the results showed that kindergartners did not simply think of respect and disrespect as opposites, in that they had a much less clear grasp of the concept of disrespect. The important point here is that kindergarten students were not knowledgeable about the concepts underlying disrespect behaviors. This suggests that formation of children's concepts of disrespect may develop later than their concepts of respect.

Kindergarten children's ratings of the respect or disrespect pictures reinforced the finding that they think differently about respect and disrespect. They indicated on a seven-point scale how respectful a behavior was if the child had looked at the respect behavior pictures. If the child had looked at the disrespect behavior pictures, he or she rated how disrespectful the behavior was. The ratings allowed us to gauge the degree to which the child identified the behaviors as representative of the concept of respect or disrespect. Ratings for all the respect behaviors were significantly higher than were ratings for all the disrespect behaviors. This means that when children looked at pictures depicting respect behaviors, they were confident in their judgments, whereas they had less confidence about the behaviors as representative of the concept of disrespect. As with their explanations, the seven-point ratings indicated overall that at the age of six, (kindergarten) children have a clear picture of what respect entails but are more variable in their explanations and judgments concerning the concept of disrespect.

First- and Second-Grade Findings. The findings for first- and second-graders indicated that an important change occurs in the concepts of respect and disrespect in transition to middle childhood.

Respect. There was greater homogeneity of responses within and between the first- and second-grade samples compared with the responses of kindergartners. Due to space limitations and general similarity of their responses between grade levels, we grouped together the data of the seven and eight year olds (first and second graders). Among the fifty children who responded to the respect behavior pictures, all said that the pictures were examples of respect behaviors. The trend toward similarity of responses was particularly noticeable for four of the five respect pictures. For example, half of the first and second graders said that respect was shown by taking good care of a pet. Eight children expressed the same concept by using a negative example, that is, it showed respect not to harm a pet. Sixteen children said that asking for permission before you use another person's possessions is an example of a respect behavior. For the same picture, eight children said that "you don't take things" was their concept of respect behavior. We do not believe these responses were simply the opposite of saying, "It shows respect to ask before using another's possessions." Rather, it seemed that these children were conveying the concept that it is respectful not to steal. Six children, in their responses to the "asking permission" respect picture, thought that the most salient feature of respect conveyed was the use of polite language ("May I use your . . ."), not that permission was sought.

A rule-specific explanation was used by twenty-eight of fifty children for the respect behavior, "Gallant shares the groups' supplies." These twenty-eight children said the concept of respect was, "He's sharing." Eight children attributed his respect behavior to a personality trait: "He's nice." The respect behavior conveyed in the picture and caption, "Watch out for these branches," elicited the most similarity of responses among any of the five respect behaviors. Forty-four children responded that "to protect your friends or others" conveyed respect. Their use of the word *protect* meant to safeguard well-being, which indicated to us that these children felt an obligation to others. This kind of sense of duty seemed to be motivated by an affective relationship between the children and others.

The fifth and last picture depicting respect behavior was of a boy sitting in a typical classroom at a desk. His hand was raised, as were the hands of some other children sitting close to him. The caption read, "Gallant waits to be called on." There was little consensus among children's responses to, "Why is this a respect behavior?" The modal response (by ten children) was, "You're supposed to raise your hand." These responses showed that for them, respect was related to the rule-specific classroom activity of raising hands, that is, it is respectful to comply with classroom rules. A number of children said that "waiting" was the most important concept related to respect, but they interpreted the meaning of "waiting" differently. Ten responses equated "waiting" with "not shouting out." These children said that respect behavior was shown by the inhibition of shouting.

These children must have practiced restraint themselves, because it would be difficult for seven- and eight-year olds otherwise to infer that their classmates were suppressing a desire to shout out when their hands were raised. So for these ten children, control of personal behavior was the concept of respect behavior that was clearest. Eight students said that waiting was related to "waiting your turn." The most important idea in this concept is that "a turn" is a shared commodity and that the respectful individual must wait until a turn is given. "Waiting patiently" was said to be the concept of respect behavior for six children. Their concept of respect combined the idea and behavior of self-control (waiting) with a positive emotion (patience). These six children conceived that calm patience in waiting to be called on in class was the key to respect behavior. This was in strong contrast to the ten children who said "waiting and not shouting out" was the principal concept of respect. The behavioral outcome was the same for "waiting patiently" and "waiting and not calling out," but the general deportment and emotional states of the two groups of children would be different. Because of their heightened emotional state when "waiting and not calling out," some children might experience stronger feelings of disappointment, frustration, and anger when they were not called on, compared with children who viewed respect as "waiting patiently."

Disrespect. Overall, the responses to the pictures by first and second graders depicting disrespect behavior were more variable than responses to the respect behavior pictures. For example, in the pet disrespect behavior picture, a boy was holding a goldfish in the palm of his hand. The goldfish bowl and water could be seen sitting on a nearby table. The boy (Goofus) said to his assembled friends, "Take it. It's fun to feel them flop around." Twelve children said that the boy's behavior did not show disrespect. Twelve said it was disrespect behavior to put the life of a pet into danger. Another six children said that it was the pet that showed a disrespect behavior because the pet might injure the boy who was holding it.

Comments about the picture with the caption of, "Goofus shouts out the answers in class" also varied. Four children said the behavior was not representative of disrespect. Most of the ideas generated by the forty-six children who said the picture was an example of disrespect behavior were negative examples. This seemed to us to show that these children could express disrespect behaviors only as the opposites of respect behavior. It once again demonstrated a developmental gap in expression of vocabulary and thinking about situations involving disrespect in comparison to the language and thought for respect behaviors. Ten first and second graders said the disrespect behavior was related to rule-specific classroom conduct, for example, "He's supposed to raise his hand," "He should wait to be called on," and "It's a rule to raise your hand." The concept of shouting was the reason the behavior "shouting out the answer" showed disrespect to ten children. Four children said that the behavior showed disrespect because it violated the rule that "you're supposed to give people a chance to think." Four other children recognized that if one child shouted out the answer, other children could not be called on to give their answers and would lose their opportunity to have a turn.

Not seeking permission was the disrespect behavior that elicited the most uniform responses among first and second graders. Twenty-two children said that it was disrespectful to use another's possessions without permission. Other concepts of disrespect for this situation ("Goofus uses his father's guitar without asking") pertained to the object itself that was being used without permission. Although there was no "value" word attached to the guitar, children said it was a disrespect behavior because the guitar had special meaning for the father, it could be broken, it was an antique, or it was expensive. We think that for the children who gave these responses, using other people's things without permission is not disrespectful. Rather, for them, the idea of asking or not asking permission depended on the value of the object and how carefully they treated it. This distinction most likely comes from training at home, which is in conflict with school rules such as, "Don't use others' things without asking the owner first." Four children said that using something without a parent's permission is a disrespect behavior because it violates their parents' expectations. The example they gave was, "Parents want you to leave their stuff alone." Only two children in all the first- and second-grade interviews said that "he'll be punished" was the reason they were motivated not to use others' things without permission. This illustrated, as had the kindergarten data, that disrespect was not related to fear of punishment.

An example of disrespect defined as a lack of respect, was found in response to a picture of classmates working together on a project. In the picture, Goofus took glue out of a girl's hand while saying, "This is my glue. Find your own!" Of the fifty participants responding to this picture, only two did not think the scene showed a disrespect behavior. The other forty-eight children identified this situation as an example of disrespect behavior. Of these, thirty-eight students said that the reason it was an example of disrespect was that the boy was not showing a respect behavior. That is, most first and second graders again used negative rather than positive examples to explain their ideas of not sharing. This indicates to us that these children lacked vocabulary and a concept for this specific disrespect behavior. None of the children spontaneously said, for example, that the behavior showed selfishness. The most common response of the first and second graders to

NEW DIRECTIONS FOR CHILD AND ADOLESCENT DEVELOPMENT • DOI: 10.1002/cad

this situation was, "He's supposed to share." This was a negative example, that is, a violation of the rule-specific behavior of sharing. The only positive examples given for why Goofus's behavior represented disrespect were: "He's being mean" (eight students) and "People will think he's mean" (two students). "Mean" for these children was more akin to the personality trait of contemptible than common or ignoble. Being mean also reflects an emotional aspect of the concept of disrespect. The response, "People will think he's mean," represented the first occurrence in all the interviews whereby character traits inferred from an observable behavior may result in a misinterpretation of a person's true character. Five children said, "He doesn't want to share," and two said, "He could share, but doesn't." Both of these responses focused on volition or the intent of behavior. These seven children conveyed the idea that the boy had no motivation to share and that the lack of motivation showed a disrespect behavior. Other responses to this item were, "Have to share with friends," "It belongs to the school, not him," and "You shouldn't yell at others." In sum, there was wide variation in how children explained the behavior of not sharing.

In contrast to the preceding variability, there was general agreement among first and second graders in response to the picture in which Gallant said, "Watch out for those branches." Forty-four of fifty students related the behavior in this situation to the concept of the need to protect friends and others. Children tended not to verbalize their ideas related to an opposite concept. The caption for the disrespect behavior was, "Goofus lets the door swing shut on the person behind him." Although children said the picture and caption were an example of disrespect behavior, responses were varied and ambiguous as to why the behavior might show disrespect. It was clear to us that disregard for other people as a concept linked to disrespect behavior could not be meaningfully expressed by seven- and eight-year old children in our sample. This led us to believe that the concept of "disregard for people" had not yet developed into a notion of disrespect behavior by second grade (age eight). Eight children said the situation represented disrespect behavior because the door could cause injury. The other forty-two explanations were so varied that no more than two children gave the same response. Examples of children's thinking about this situation included, "It might make someone feel bad," "He let his friend in, but not others," "The person has to open the door all by themselves," and "Maybe they're carrying lots of things."

Age-Level Comparisons. First- and second-grade students also rated how well each respect behavior item and each disrespect behavior item represented its concept. As was the case among the kindergartners, ratings for all respect behavior items were higher than all disrespect behavior items. These differences were statistically significant for the pet situation and for the situation of asking permission to use another person's possession. This was evidence that first- and second-grade children were more confident about why behaviors were respectful than they were about knowing why behaviors are disrespectful, as was also the case among kindergarten children. The most dramatic difference between the kindergarten (six-year olds) and first- and second-grade children (seven- and eight-years old) was that first and second graders were much more likely to consolidate their concepts underlying why a respect behavior was thought to be a respect behavior, for four of the five situations presented to them. Age differences within disrespect behaviors were most noticeable when children responded to the situation of asking permission to use another person's possessions. Among all the kindergartners, first graders, and second graders we interviewed, expression of clear-cut concepts related to disrespect behaviors appeared to lag behind the development of concepts related to respect behaviors. This was seen in responses about respect that tended to be more similar than dissimilar, whereas responses about disrespect were more variable and tended to be explained with negative examples (defining disrespect by what it was not). Overall, we concluded that children's understanding for the concept of respect was clearer than their understanding of the concept of disrespect.

Conclusion

The preceding data were some of our first findings about the developmental trajectories of respect and disrespect among American children. A subsequent report will detail the results of our interviews with third through eighth graders at the same school. We believe that by virtue of their being reared in the same community, the thinking of these American children was more similar than dissimilar. This is not to say that we do not appreciate what makes each child unique, and indeed there were many individual differences in children's explanations of both respect and disrespect behaviors. But this research also uncovered general patterns at two age levels that we believe are suggestive of normative behavior, thought, and feeling in an American context, relevant to the development of the concepts of respect and disrespect.

Piaget (1932) and Vygotsky (1962) directed our attention to how we can proceed with the scientific study of respect and disrespect in children: by listening to children. Vygotsky in particular made it clear that children's language is the window to their cognitive processing. We were also able to draw on ideas from more recent approaches, including information processing models, and theories that view behavior, emotion, and cognition as interrelated rather than mutually exclusive domains of development. Clearly we must integrate the behavioral, attitudinal, and conceptual aspects of respect and disrespect in our ongoing research.

Our own data confirmed that as in Piaget's view (1932), there is a unilateral form of respect related to compliance. Our findings also indicated, however, that by the time children enter kindergarten, both respect and disrespect are already multidimensional, multicontextual, and situation-specific concepts. As has been shown in every other chapter in this volume, there is a cultural basis for children's conceptualization, and this leads us to question Piaget's distinction between unilateral (early childhood) and mutual (middle childhood) respect. Vygotsky's theory (1962) tells us that we must understand how adults and other agents of socialization guide children in culture-related activities that may lead to culture-specific concepts of respect and disrespect. But both of these seminal theories leave it to us and future researchers to determine what develops at what ages, and to what degree the developmental pathways of respect and disrespect are culture specific or universal.

The data reported in this chapter suggest general patterns in the developmental trajectories of the two concepts. For example, we found more uniformity in children's explanations of respect than of disrespect. We also found more variability in the responses of kindergartners than among first and second graders. These and other trends are only preliminary findings, but they make it clear that the development of the concepts of respect and disrespect is a more complex process than Piaget had suggested. Ongoing analysis of our data through the eighth grade will help reveal what more emerges in middle childhood and into the transition to adolescence besides mutual respect (Piaget, 1932). We believe that our research and that of the other contributors to this volume will show that respect and disrespect both begin with "the word" and end in culture.

References

Dollard, J., and others. *Frustration and Aggression.* New Haven, Conn.: Yale University Press, 1939.

Kohlberg, L. "The Development of Children's Orientations Toward a Moral Order: I. Sequence in the Development of Moral Thought." *Vita Humana,* 1963, 6, 11–36.

Lewis, M., and Haviland-Jones, J. M. *Handbook of Emotions.* (2nd ed.) New York: Guilford Press, 2000.

Nguyen, K. "The Concepts of Respect and Disrespect Among College Students." Unpublished master's thesis, Southeastern Louisiana University, 2006.

Piaget, J. *The Moral Judgment of the Child.* Orlando, Fla.: Harcourt, 1932.

Shwalb, B., and others. "The Meaning of Respect in Childhood and Adolescence." Paper presented at the biennial meetings of the Society for Adolescent Research, San Francisco, 2006.

Thorndike, E. *The Fundamentals of Learning.* New York: Teachers College Press, 1932.

Vygotsky, L. *Thought and Language* (E. Hanfmann and G. Vakar, Eds.). Cambridge, Mass.: MIT Press, 1962.

Yelsma, P., and Yelsma, J. "Self-Esteem and Social Respect Within the High School." *Journal of Social Psychology,* 1998, 138, 431–441.

BARBARA J. SHWALB *is on the faculty of the Psychology Department at Southeastern Louisiana University.*

DAVID W. SHWALB *is on the faculty of the Psychology Department at Southeastern Louisiana University.*

In addition to work on respect and disrespect, the Shwalbs conduct cross-cultural research on parental belief systems, social-personality development in school setttings, and cooperative learning.

7

This volume overall provides a compelling description of what respect entails and how it functions and emerges in childhood and adolescence. This construct requires further conceptual clarification and study across cultures. The strength of this volume lies in its cultural perspective and diverse empirical approaches.

Respect in Children Across Cultures

Jin Li

Respect is one of those things that we recognize, feel, and want, but find hard to define and even harder to study. Perhaps this very state is one reason that there has been so little research on respect. Since Seligman's American Psychological Association presidential address (1999) called on the field to study positive psychology, there has been increased attention to respect as part of positive human psychology. This volume represents a genuine advance in this new research direction.

Together the previous chapters in this volume contribute to our understanding of what respect may be, how it may function, and how it may emerge in children and adolescents. Some chapters present the authors' own empirical findings, and others review previous research and offer conceptual discussions. All chapters adopt the important perspective of culture and collectively show the complexity of respect. In this chapter, I highlight the construct of respect as gleaned from this volume and discuss the influence of culture on the development of respect in children. I conclude by suggesting some future research directions.

Construct of Respect

This volume, drawing on limited research from the past, seems to describe respect as a social/attitudinal construct that guides people's social behavior toward others and regulates relationships (Frei and Shaver, 2002). Respect is therefore considered an important component of a person's social competence (see Chapter Five, this volume). Respect is shown to four targets: two

NEW DIRECTIONS FOR CHILD AND ADOLESCENT DEVELOPMENT, no. 114, Winter 2006 © Wiley Periodicals, Inc.
Published online in Wiley InterScience (www.interscience.wiley.com) • DOI: 10.1002/cad.177

kinds of people, one's community, and nonhuman lives or objects. The first type of people who receive respect are authority figures, including parents and other kin and nonkin elders, teachers, and religious practitioners (Chapters Two through Six address respect for authority). These people receive respect in relation to their roles, older generational status, higher social position, or power within the family and society. The second kind of people to whom respect is shown are one's peers (Chapters Five and Six) on the grounds of their equal status, mutuality, and reciprocity. People also express respect toward their group and community (Chapter Two). Finally, people may give respect to nonhuman recipients (for example, goldfish and guitar, as shown in Chapter Six). However, the two kinds of people, authority figures and peers, are the main targets to whom respect is shown in most research.

When people show respect, there seems to be a set of behavioral, linguistic, and symbolic norms that convey respect. Behavioral norms toward authority figures include receptivity (attentiveness, listening, not talking back, and following), yielding, politeness, obedience, and compliance. Chapters Two and Three describe these behavioral norms clearly. With regard to peers, respectful behavior entails sharing, turn taking, self-control, following rules, and not hurting others. The data that Shwalb and Shwalb present in Chapter Six address these behaviors. Linguistic and symbolic norms are structural devices to allow individuals to express respect in a given culture. For example, both Japanese and Southeast Asian languages have honorific speech and ritualized bodily gestures that people acquire and use to display respect toward others.

Although respect is mostly a social-attitudinal construct, it also involves affect. Research by Bankston and Hidalgo (Chapter Three, as well as the literature review by Sugie, Shwalb, and Shwalb (Chapter Four) point to closeness and warmth with the respected person (for example, mothers). Research by Cohen and collaborators (Chapter Five) emphasizes peer admiration and liking, while Harwood, Yalcinkaya, Citlak, and Leyendecker (Chapter Two) highlight family honor and ethnic pride through respect toward one's parents and ethnic group within a larger immigrant country. Finally, in defining what respect (and disrespect) may mean to young children, Shwalb and Shwalb describe that a sense of duty may underlie some children's understanding of respect. Harwood, Yalcinkaya, Citlak, and Leyendecker also document that instilling a sense of duty and responsibility is part of respect valued by Puerto Rican and Turkish mothers.

The final component of the respect construct concerns the functions of respect. Each of the targets of respect seems to be linked to a set of positive functions that respect serves. For authority within the family, respect generates harmony and good parent-child relationships. All chapters that address respect toward authority indicate that respect is important for family life. Respect for family elders promotes family cohesion. Because family structure is hierarchical, duties and responsibilities differ among the generations. When a family is cohesive, children feel emotionally attached to and protected by their family, which in turn contributes to better social adjustment and higher school achievement. Chapter Three by Bankston and Hidalgo speaks to these functions of respect clearly. Respect for teachers also seems to be linked to better school adjustment and higher achievement. As Bankston and Hidalgo point out, American schools are hierarchical in nature. Respect developed at home can readily transfer to authority at school, which promotes learning and achievement. Similarly, Cohen and others find that while U.S. children acknowledge obedience as their behavioral manifestation of respect for teachers, their Chinese peers exert greater effort in learning to show their respect to their teachers (Hsueh and others, 2005). It follows that both behavioral tendencies of respect may facilitate children's learning and achievement.

Respect for peers promotes friendship and better peer relationships in general, which also helps children develop better social competence. Research by Cohen and others provides evidence for this function of respect. Finally, respect for one's ethnic community strengthens one's ethnic identity, an essential developmental task among ethnic youth. Research by Harwood, Yalcinkaya, Citlak, and Leyendecker shows maternal beliefs relevant to this function of respect.

In sum, respect seems to be directed particularly toward authority in the family and school, on the one hand, and peers, on the other hand. There is a clear set of behavioral, linguistic, and symbolic norms that people use to express respect. This volume also showed that affect is a part of respect and that respect leads to a host of positive outcomes in children and families.

Research Approach

The researchers in this volume represent diverse empirical approaches to tap three aspects of respect: definition, function, and parental socialization goals. For the first aim, Cohen and others (also reported by Hsueh and others, 2005) used open-ended methods to elicit elementary school children's definitions of respect; then they used children's definitions to probe why and how they would show respect toward teachers and peers. Similarly, Shwalb and Shwalb used picture scenarios and captions to explore how children might define respect and how confident they would feel about their judgment. For the second aim of function, Cohen and others used rating scales to assess how children's respect influenced their peer relations. For the third aim of socialization goals, Harwood, Yalcinkaya, Citlak, and Leyendecker used interviews to analyze child-rearing goals from immigrant mothers of young children in the United States and Germany. These diverse methods produced informative data on the various components of respect as viewed by different cultural and age groups.

NEW DIRECTIONS FOR CHILD AND ADOLESCENT DEVELOPMENT • DOI: 10.1002/cad

Cultural Similarities and Variations

A strong point of this volume is that all researchers seriously consider culture as a source of influence. The wider cultural groups that this volume covers shed important light on the concept of respect. There are cultural similarities as well as variations. Two cultural similarities seem apparent. First is the fact that respect is a positive social/attitudinal construct that children develop and express in their social interactions with authority and peers. The second similarity is that respect, regardless of culture and ethnicity, seems to promote good authority-child relationships, peer relationships, children's socioemotional well-being, and school achievement.

There also appear to be more similarities among the non-Anglo cultural groups. If we set the research by Cohen and others and by Shwalb and Shwalb aside for a moment and look at Chapters Two through Four, we could see greater similarities among these cultural groups. A key pattern is that respect is widely and strongly directed at parents and kin elders. It is therefore reasonable to conclude that respect is an important family and child-rearing dimension in these non-Western cultural groups.

Not only is respect essential for family life across these groups, but there are also concrete cultural devices in place, such as honorific language, ritualized bodily gestures (for example, bowing and holding both hands together in front of the respected person), and other behavioral norms (for instance, remaining calm and sweet in the presence of elders among Puerto Rican children). These devices enable children to acquire the concept of respect for family, and this socialization continues from generation to generation.

Finally, these non-Anglo groups share a stronger affect, warmth, and closeness to family when children and adults talk about respect toward their kin elders. These respect-based affects generate a sense of family bonding and smooth functioning despite the necessity of family hierarchy. Family hierarchy may be balanced through respect-related feelings by "providing differentiation between family members," on the one hand, and achieving "intimacy, interdependence, and proximity," on the other (Harwood, Yalcinkaya, Citlak, and Leyendecker). This delicate balance may be the very key to survival and maintenance of these non-Anglo cultural groups. Therefore, the family may be the most essential context in which children develop respect.

Despite these similarities, there seem to be some clear differences in how children define and express respect toward teachers and peers between American and Asian cultures. Cohen and others mention that both American and Chinese children respect teachers. Younger American children's respect for teachers is also confirmed by Shwalb and Shwalb. However, American children's behavioral expression of respect for teachers is to obey them or to follow rules, whereas Chinese children work harder in their learning to show respect for teachers.

NEW DIRECTIONS FOR CHILD AND ADOLESCENT DEVELOPMENT • DOI: 10.1002/cad

Similarly, as Cohen and others showed, both American and Chinese children acknowledge respect for their peers. However, a greater number of Chinese than American children named admiration, a clearly affective construct, as their reason for their peer respect. American children predominantly gave reciprocity as their reason for peer respect (Hsueh and others, 2005). More significant, Chinese children's respect (defined more as peer admiration) positively predicted their friendship making and peer relations, while American children's respect did not have this predictivity. Shwalb and Shwalb also provide evidence that American children's respect is more defined by rights and rule-based moral principles as expressed in sharing, turn taking, not hurting others, and not using properties that do not belong to oneself. It seems that respect among American children may be more based on moral principles than on affect.

Further Differentiation of Respect

The research and discussion in this volume will stimulate further theoretical work on respect. One remaining issue is whether respect is just a catchall concept indicating a virtuous quality of a person, or whether it is a distinct construct from notions such as caring, kindness, and friendliness. Based on the research in this volume and my own research on this topic, I would argue that respect is a distinct construct.

As stated on the outset, respect is a social/attitudinal construct. Its social nature indicates that it cannot occur just within the individual; it requires that the target person be present for one to show respect. Therefore, social context is a prerequisite for respect. The attitudinal nature of respect does not point to a personality trait because a trait is an enduring quality of a person (Funder, 2001). But a person can feel or not feel respect and show or not show respect to another person. Respect is thus other-dependent. Although respect may involve behaviors that are caring, kind, and friendly, it is unlikely to be limited to the behavioral dispositions. I venture to say that respect is not only a social/attitudinal construct, but it is also an emotion, and more likely a self-conscious emotion.

In a recent article (Li and Fischer, forthcoming), I distinguished between two kinds of respect that may be found across cultures: *ought-respect* and *affect-respect,* both extended to another person. Ought-respect refers to the kind of respect everyone deserves based on political, moral, and legal considerations in society. This kind of respect is strongly endorsed in the West. The statement that no one should be discriminated against based on race, origin, skin color, cultural background, social status, or sexual orientation is a rights-based moral principle that underlies ought-respect. However, ought-respect is not generated in a specific social context or relationship because it is for everyone. This kind of respect does not vary due to temporal or contextual particularities. Therefore, it is not expressed as an emotion under normal circumstances. Nor does ought-respect generate specific physical or

NEW DIRECTIONS FOR CHILD AND ADOLESCENT DEVELOPMENT • DOI: 10.1002/cad

bodily gestures and behaviors, as do typical emotions. Given that ought-respect is tied to a rights-based moral principle and mandated by law and it is not person or relationship specific, ought-respect is a more reason-based social, moral, and attitudinal construct. The research in this volume by Cohen and others and by Shwalb and Shwalb may have tapped this kind of respect in American children because affect was not the main concern (but sharing, fairness, and rule following are) in children's understanding and expression of respect.

Respect for teachers as authority figures may also lean toward ought-respect. This may be particularly true in the West. Respect may be directed at what the teacher represents officially rather than who the teacher is as a person. Respect is more for the position and power that gives the person authority, not vice versa. Because authority here is viewed more as institutional property, it is fundamentally impersonal. Respect for authority is more tied to the regulations, law, or policies rather than those who enforce them, such as police (we obey the law but not the officer who happens to be in the uniform enforcing the law). This may explain why the majority of American children but not their Chinese peers, as Cohen and others note, believed that showing respect to teachers is to obey them. Obeying what the institution of school mandates through teachers is consistent with lawfulness and good citizenship.

Affect-respect, in contrast, is mostly an emotion, and it is more likely a self-conscious emotion that is generated in a specific social context or relationship. This affect arises when one recognizes the good qualities of another, such as moral, intellectual, athletic, artistic, and other personal qualities and achievement that the self desires, is in the process of acquiring, or already possesses to some degree. We call it a self-conscious emotion because of the likelihood that the self may identify with such a person and is reminded of the self's own good qualities. However, the self may not regard the level and degree of his or her own qualities as being as high or extensive as the respected person. The recognition of this gap may be the foundation for one to long for, accept, follow, and emulate the respected person.

Affect-respect can be observed when a sports fan meets his or her beloved hero, or a college student who has been studying and memorizing Maya Angelou's poems since sixth grade finally meets her, or an admirer meets Nelson Mandela. Affect-respect is not limited to the extreme experience with the greatest individuals in the world, but people can feel affect-respect toward a teenager who is on the high school honor roll or is dedicated to volunteer work. Affect-respect does not require mutuality as a condition as Piaget (1962) would argue for respect among peers. Children feel this kind of respect toward certain people not because they expect the other to extend this kind of respect in return. In fact, self-awareness of our lesser qualities prevents us from expecting such mutuality.

Affect-respect is likely to do a great deal of psychological good to the self. First, it may underlie the functional mechanism of role models, a common human psychological phenomenon. A role model for the self is neces-

NEW DIRECTIONS FOR CHILD AND ADOLESCENT DEVELOPMENT • DOI: 10.1002/cad

sarily someone the self admires and desires to emulate, and it is one positive possible self (Markus and Nurius, 1986). A child who identifies a role model has a clear, concrete, tangible, real human figure in mind. The fact that a person is identified as a role model for the self indicates that he or she has some understanding of the basic quality, merit, and achievements of that role model. Identification of a role model also necessarily indicates at least some self-awareness of the discrepancy between the self and the role model, and possibly also ways to narrow the discrepancy. Second, each time the self is made aware of the target person, the self may experience affect-respect, a highly positive emotion that also makes the self feel good about himself or herself. Finally, affect-respect may generate strong motivation for action and behavior that propels the self toward acquiring the qualities of the respected person. In sum, feeling affect-respect for a person may motivate the self eventually to become such a person.

Research by Cohen and others reported in this volume and Hsueh and others (2005) shows that Chinese children most often named admiration as a feature for their peer respect, while few American children in their research named this feature. This finding may explain why respect of Chinese, but not American, children mediated their social competence and mutual friends. These findings make sense considering that children's social competence and friendship making depend strongly on their emotional bonding with other children. If respect is mostly experienced as peer admiration, affect-respect should be linked to Chinese children's social outcomes. By contrast, it should not be surprising that respect construed and experienced with a lack of emotionality by American children does not predict social outcomes.

Chinese children also indicated that working harder is their way of showing respect for teachers (compared to American children's obedience, in Hsueh and others, 2005). Effort is a well-noted personal virtue in learning for the Chinese (Li, 2004), and teachers are regarded not just as institutional figures but, more important, as learning models for children (Li, 2001). It is quite possible that hard work is a behavioral manifestation of children's affect-respect toward teachers who are not merely obeyed but also emulated as role models. Thus, ought-respect and affect-respect may coexist.

Finally, research on respect toward parents and kin elders by Harwood, Yalcinkaya, Citlak, and Leyendecker, as well as the literature reviews by Bankston and Hidalgo and Sugie, Shwalb, and Shwalb, are relevant to the two kinds of respect as well. The nature of children's respect toward parents and kin elders may be similar to that for teachers in Chinese culture. In fact, Chinese teachers are traditionally viewed as parental figures. Family elders are not regarded as impersonal authorities, but as authority whose power and legitimacy lie in the kin elders' moral guidance, care, and emotional commitment to their children. Children's respect may not be purely based on affect because parents and kin elders are still authorities they must accept (therefore, obedience is expected). However, the weight of their respect may lean toward affect nonetheless. Children may respect their parents by acknowledgment of parental knowledge, wisdom, and guidance, which children know they lack. They may also respect parents to express gratitude for parental sacrifice. Finally, they may truly admire their parents as a source of inspiration for the kind of people they hope to become.

Future Directions

Because respect as a construct is still being conceptualized, we would benefit much from research devoted to clarifying the construct itself. Hsueh and others (2005) offer a promising direction. I (Li, 2006) have also collected over two hundred words and expressions in Chinese on both ought-respect and affect-respect. After narrowing these words down for core meanings, we can examine how groups of meanings are organized to reveal the whole construct of respect in Chinese. Researchers can do similar work in other cultures. For example, Shwalb and others (2006) collected over a thousand examples of respect (and well over a thousand examples of disrespect in a parallel study) from American school teachers and parents as the basis of a factor-analytic study on the meanings of respect and disrespect. This type of research can provide a conceptual map of respect for each culture. Such culture-level models can help us generate specific research questions about how people define respect toward what kind of people in what social contexts and how people show respect. Once we know what respect is and how it functions in people's lives, we will be better equipped to examine how children develop respect across cultures. Shwalb and Shwalb have a good method to probe American children's understanding of respect, and Harwood, Yalcinkaya, Citlak, and Leyendecker present valuable data on immigrant parents' socialization goals for their children in developing respect.

Respect is a very important research topic. Although researchers have rarely studied it, this volume marks a significant advance. As we gain a better understanding of respect, we can hope to give and receive respect in a world that needs respect more than ever.

References

Frei, J. R., and Shaver, P. R. "Respect in Close Relationships: Prototype Definition, Self-Report Assessment, and Initial Correlates." *Personal Relationships*, 2002, *9*, 121–139.
Funder, D. C. *The Personality Puzzle*. (2nd ed.) New York: Norton, 2001.
Hsueh, Y., and others. "Knowing and Showing Respect: Chinese and U.S. Children's Understanding of Respect and Its Association to Their Friendships." *Journal of Psychology in Chinese Societies*, 2005, *6*(2), 229-260.
Li, J. "Chinese Conceptualization of Learning." *Ethos*, 2001, *29*, 111–137.
Li, J. "Learning as a Task and a Virtue: U.S. and Chinese Preschoolers Explain Learning." *Developmental Psychology*, 2004, *40*(4), 595–605.

Li, J. [Chinese terms referring to positive self-conscious emotions of pride, honor, respect, face, gratitude, and humility.] Unpublished raw data, 2006.

Li, J., and Fischer, K. W. "Respect as a Positive Self-Conscious Emotion in Westerners and Chinese People." In R. Robins, J. Tracy, and J. P. Tangney (eds.), *The Self-Conscious Emotions: Theory and Research*. New York: Guilford Press, forthcoming.

Markus, H. R., and Nurius, P. "Possible Selves." *American Psychologist*, 1986, *41*, 954–969.

Piaget, J. *The Moral Judgment of the Child* (M. Gabain, trans.). New York: Collier, 1962. (Originally published in 1932.)

Seligman, M. E. "The President's Address." *American Psychologist*, 1999, *54*, 559–562.

Shwalb, B. J., and others. "The Meaning of Respect in Childhood and Adolescence." Paper presented at the meetings of the Society for Adolescent Research, San Francisco, 2006.

JIN LI is associate professor of education and human development at Brown University. She studies children's learning beliefs, self, and self-conscious emotions across cultures.

INDEX

Back Issue/Subscription Order Form

Copy or detach and send to:

Jossey-Bass, A Wiley Imprint, 989 Market Street, San Francisco CA 94103-1741
Call or fax toll-free: Phone 888-378-2537 6:30AM–3PM PST; Fax 888-481-2665

Back Issues: Please send me the following issues at $29 each

(Important: please indicate the New Directions title initials and issue numbers—for example, "CD99" for New Directions in Child and Adolescent Development, number 99.)

_____

_____

_____

$ _____ Total for single issues

$ _____ SHIPPING CHARGES: SURFACE   Domestic   Canadian

                                   First Item $5.00 $6.00

                                   Each Add'l Item $3.00 $1.50

For next-day and second-day delivery rates, call the number listed above.

Subscriptions   Please ___ start ___ renew my subscription to *New Directions for Child and Adolescent Development* for the year 2_____ at the following rate:

     U.S.   ___ Individual $90   ___ Institutional $240

     Canada   ___ Individual $90   ___ Institutional $280

     All Others   ___ Individual $114 ___ Institutional $314

Online subscriptions are available via Wiley InterScience!

For more information about online subscriptions visit
www.wileyinterscience.com

$_____ Total single issues and subscriptions (Add appropriate sales tax for your state for single issue orders. No sales tax for U.S. subscriptions. Canadian residents, add GST for subscriptions and single issues.)

___ Payment enclosed (U.S. check or money order only)

___ VISA ___ MC ___ AmEx # _____ Exp. Date _____

Signature _____ Day Phone _____

___ Bill Me (U.S. institutional orders only. Purchase order required.)

Purchase order # _____

                 Federal Tax ID13559302   **GST 89102 8052**

Name _____

Address _____

_____

Phone _____ E-mail _____

For more information about Jossey-Bass, visit our Web site at www.josseybass.com

OTHER TITLES AVAILABLE IN THE
NEW DIRECTIONS FOR CHILD AND ADOLESCENT DEVELOPMENT SERIES
Reed W. Larson and Lene Arnett Jensen, Editors-in-Chief
William Damon, Founding Editor-in-Chief

NEW DIRECTIONS FOR CHILD AND ADOLESCENT DEVELOPMENT IS NOW AVAILABLE ONLINE AT WILEY INTERSCIENCE

What is Wiley InterScience?

Wiley InterScience is the dynamic online content service from John Wiley & Sons delivering the full text of over 300 leading scientific, technical, medical, and professional journals, plus major reference works, the acclaimed Current Protocols laboratory manuals, and even the full text of select Wiley print books online.

What are some special features of Wiley InterScience?

Wiley Interscience Alerts is a service that delivers table of contents via e-mail for any journal available on Wiley InterScience as soon as a new issue is published online.

EarlyView is Wiley's exclusive service presenting individual articles online as soon as they are ready, even before the release of the compiled print issue. These articles are complete, peer-reviewed, and citable.

CrossRef is the innovative multi-publisher reference linking system enabling readers to move seamlessly from a reference in a journal article to the cited publication, typically located on a different server and published by a different publisher.

How can I access Wiley InterScience?

Visit http://www.interscience.wiley.com.

Guest Users can browse Wiley InterScience for unrestricted access to journal tables of contents and article abstracts, or use the powerful search engine.

Registered Users are provided with a *Personal Home Page* to store and manage customized alerts, searches, and links to favorite journals and articles. Additionally, Registered Users can view free online sample issues and preview selected material from major reference works.

Licensed Customers are entitled to access full-text journal articles in PDF, with select journals also offering full-text HTML.

How do I become an Authorized User?

Authorized Users are individuals authorized by a paying Customer to have access to the journals in Wiley InterScience. For example, a university that subscribes to Wiley journals is considered to be the Customer.

Faculty, staff, and students authorized by the university to have access to those journals in Wiley InterScience are Authorized Users. Users should contact their library for information on which Wiley journals they have access to in Wiley InterScience.

ASK YOUR INSTITUTION ABOUT WILEY INTERSCIENCE TODAY!

United States Postal Service
Statement of Ownership, Management, and Circulation

1. Publication Title	2. Publication Number									3. Filing Date
New Directions For Child And Adolescent Development	1	5	2	0	_	3	2	4	7	10/1/06

4. Issue Frequency	5. Number of Issues Published Annually	6. Annual Subscription Price
Quarterly	4	$240.00

7. Complete Mailing Address of Known Office of Publication (Not printer) (Street, city, county, state, and ZIP+4)	Contact Person
	Joe Schuman
Wiley Subscription Services, Inc. at Jossey-Bass, 989 Market Street, San Francisco, CA 94103	Telephone
	(415) 782-3232

8. Complete Mailing Address of Headquarters or General Business Office of Publisher (Not printer)

Wiley Subscription Services, Inc. 111 River Street, Hoboken, NJ 07030

9. Full Names and Complete Mailing Addresses of Publisher, Editor, and Managing Editor (Do not leave blank)
Publisher (Name and complete mailing address)

Wiley Subscriptions Services, Inc., A Wiley Company at San Francisco, 989 Market Street, San Francisco, CA 94103-1741

Editor (Name and complete mailing address)

Co-Editor - Reed Larson, Dept. of Human & Community Develpmnt, Univ. of Illinois, 1105 W. Nevada St., Urbana IL 61801

Managing Editor (Name and complete mailing address)

Co-Editor - Dr. Lene Arnett Jensen, Ph.D., Assoc. Prof., Catholic University, Life Cycle Institute, Washington, DC 20064

10. Owner (Do not leave blank. If the publication is owned by a corporation, give the name and address of the corporation immediately followed by the names and addresses of all stockholders owning or holding 1 percent or more of the total amount of stock. If not owned by a corporation, give the names and addresses of the individual owners. If owned by a partnership or other unincorporated firm, give its name and address as well as those of each individual owner. If the publication is published by a nonprofit organization, give its name and address.)

Full Name	Complete Mailing Address
Wiley Subscription Services, Inc.	111 River Street, Hoboken, NJ 07030
(see attached list)	

11. Known Bondholders, Mortgagees, and Other Security Holders Owning or Holding 1 Percent or More of Total Amount of Bonds, Mortgages, or Other Securities. If none, check box ▶ ☑ None

Full Name	Complete Mailing Address
None	None

12. Tax Status (For completion by nonprofit organizations authorized to mail at nonprofit rates) (Check one)
The purpose, function, and nonprofit status of this organization and the exempt status for federal income tax purposes:
☐ Has Not Changed During Preceding 12 Months
☐ Has Changed During Preceding 12 Months (Publisher must submit explanation of change with this statement)

13. Publication Title New Directions For Child And Adolescent Development	Issue Date for Circulation Data Below Summer 2006

15. Extent and Nature of Circulation			Average No. Copies Each Issue During Preceding 12 Months	No. Copies of Single Issue Published Nearest to Filing Date
a. Total Number of Copies (Net press run)			846	863
b. Paid and/or Requested Circulation	(1)	Paid/Requested Outside-County Mail Subscriptions Stated on Form 3541. (Include advertiser's proof and exchange copies)	247	250
	(2)	Paid In-County Subscriptions Stated on Form 3541 (Include advertiser's proof and exchange copies)	0	0
	(3)	Sales Through Dealers and Carriers, Street Vendors, Counter Sales, and Other Non-USPS Paid Distribution	0	0
	(4)	Other Classes Mailed Through the USPS	0	0
c. Total Paid and/or Requested Circulation [Sum of 15b. (1), (2),(3),and (4)]		▶	247	250
d. Free Distribution by Mail (Samples, complimentary, and other free)	(1)	Outside-County as Stated on Form 3541	0	0
	(2)	In-County as Stated on Form 3541	0	0
	(3)	Other Classes Mailed Through the USPS	0	0
e. Free Distribution Outside the Mail (Carriers or other means)			56	61
f. Total Free Distribution (Sum of 15d. and 15e.)		▶	56	61
g. Total Distribution (Sum of 15c. and 15f)		▶	303	311
h. Copies not Distributed			543	552
i. Total (Sum of 15g. and h.)		▶	846	863
j. Percent Paid and/or Requested Circulation (15c. divided by 15g. times 100)			82%	80%

16. Publication of Statement of Ownership
☑ Publication required. Will be printed in the __Winter 2006__ issue of this publication. ☐ Publication not required.

17. Signature and Title of Editor, Publisher, Business Manager, or Owner	Date
Susan E. Lewis, VP & Publisher - Periodicals _Susan (Lewis)_	10/01/06

I certify that all information furnished on this form is true and complete. I understand that anyone who furnishes false or misleading information on this form or who omits material or information requested on the form may be subject to criminal sanctions (including fines and imprisonment) and/or civil sanctions (including civil penalties).